It's Time To H.E.A.L.

Helping • Educating • Answering • Learning

TRAFFORD

USA • Canada • UK • Ireland

Disclaimer:

· This Publication contains the story of the author. It is intended to provide helpful information only. It is sold with the understanding that the author and publisher do not dispense medical advice or prescribe the use of any technique as a form of treatment for physical or medical problems without the advice of a competent professional, either directly or indirectly. In the event that you choose to use any of the information in this book for yourself, the author and publisher assume no responsibility for your actions.

Note for Librarians: A cataloguing record for this book is available from Library and Archives Canada at www.collectionscanada.ca/amicus/index-e.html
ISBN 1-4120-6247-0

Printed in Victoria, BC, Canada. Printed on paper with minimum 30% recycled fibre. Trafford's print shop runs on "green energy" from solar, wind and other environmentally-friendly power sources.

Offices in Canada, USA, Ireland and UK
This book was published *on-demand* in cooperation with Trafford Publishing. On-demand publishing is a unique process and service of making a book available for retail sale to the public taking advantage of on-demand manufacturing and Internet marketing. On-demand publishing includes promotions, retail sales, manufacturing, order fulfilment, accounting and collecting royalties on behalf of the author.

Book sales for North America and international:
Trafford Publishing, 6E–2333 Government St.,
Victoria, BC V8T 4P4 CANADA
phone 250 383 6864 (toll-free 1 888 232 4444)
fax 250 383 6804; email to orders@trafford.com
Book sales in Europe:
Trafford Publishing (UK) Limited, 9 Park End Street, 2nd Floor
Oxford, UK OX1 1HH UNITED KINGDOM
phone 44 (0)1865 722 113 (local rate 0845 230 9601)
facsimile 44 (0)1865 722 868; info.uk@trafford.com
Order online at:
trafford.com/ 05-1148

It's Time To H.E.A.L.

Helping • Educating • Answering • Learning

A NEW WAY TO LIVE YOUR LIFE... AFTER ABUSE

Heather Mesaric

I dedicate this book to all the survivors of this world—
may they "find their voice."

Acknowledgements

A passionate thanks to God for sending His angels to me when I needed them the most. I owe them my life. I also want to thank God for always being my guide and companion throughout my life, even when I did not know He was there for me, and for being alongside me during the long and vigorous hours it took for me to write this book. I truly believe that I am only the catalyst for telling the world what God wants everyone to know about the healing process and I thank Him for choosing me to do His work.

A devoted thank you to my husband Danny, who insistently believed in this process and continuously encouraged me to follow my heart. He constantly supported me while I went through all the various emotions and feelings that I experienced during the countless stages of recovery and stuck by me during the rough times in my healing process.

An extra special thanks to my three daughters Julie, Jenn, and Sarah and my son Daniel for letting me give them a life of love and dedication. For letting me learn how to be a good mom, even when I didn't think I knew how. Most of all for understanding the long hours it took for me to write this book. **A loving thanks** to my daughter Jenn for volunteering her computer skills and my daughter Julie for assisting with reading and editing the proof copy of the book, in order to make this book perfect in every way possible.

A heartfelt thank you to my first husband Robert (Bob) for being a great father to our two wonderful daughters and for understanding that in order for me to heal completety, I needed to take a direction in life that did not include him, which ultimately allowed me to venture onto the path of recovery and healing.

A loving thank you to my sister Dolly and brother Terry. My sister for being there when I needed someone to talk to about what I was feeling, especially in the wee hours of the night. My brother for trying to "save me" all those times when we were kids.

A sincere thanks to my best friend Deb McKague who was the one person who helped me to initiate my journey of healing. Without her I would not have made the important steps that would change my life forever.

A fond thanks to my dearest friend of all times Kathy McLeod for keeping our friendship alive and well for over 30 years and for being a woman whom I've always admired and respected. Above all, for being an individual who has spent her life going after her dreams. She has shown me with her own life experiences and struggles that obstacles can't keep you down unless you let them, and that, *your dreams are always worth going after.* She has been my inspiration since the day we first met.

Thank you to Deb Headley for her love and friendship which means so much to me. Without her support, this book would not have been written. For many hours over the phone, I read to her each and every chapter of my first draft. She truly is an angel sent from God.

A special thank you goes to the following friends for reading and giving their input on how to improve the book: Michelle Flynn, Ewa Magda, Robert Young and Dave Jull. **A genuine thank you to Dave Jull** for encouraging me to pursue my dream of writing this book. He kept me motivated by asking me, "How's the book coming along?" I thank him for being an encouraging colleague for whom I hold the utmost respect. He is a man that is appreciated and cherished by those who have had the privilege of being able to work with him and I am very grateful to be one of those lucky people.

A warm thank you goes to Tamara Der-Ohanian for contacting a special friend and asking her if she would take on the task of editing my book.

An enormous thank you goes to Daryl Wood who helped me edit my book. Without her constant understanding, insight and guidance I'd still have a draft and no finished product. She helped to make my dream a reality.

A generous thank you goes out to all the hardworking, dedicated and understanding employees from Trafford Publishing who spent many hours assembling my book. They really listened to my suggestions and worked their magic in order to make my dream of having a published book come true.

Contents Page

*W*hat H.E.A.L. Means To Me...

Helping – To destroy the barriers and stigma that are associated with abuse by tearing down the walls that prevent us from seeing the world in a positive way.

Educating – Oneself to allow the doors to be opened that were once locked or barricaded; and by developing skills that will enlighten the world around you.

Answering – Those difficult questions that burn within and finding the answers that were never provided by the world around you. Discovering answers that lie deep within you, like a buried treasure, waiting to be found.

Learning – To rebuild your life, one step at a time; by learning to discover, that you are not alone and that you do, "**have a voice.**"

*I*ntroduction

We need to continue to learn more about the abuse that happens to innocent people behind closed doors and help them discover a way to open the door. We need to help them find their voice in order to make the abuse stop. Finding your voice when you are abused, confused, angry, and/or alone can be scary and difficult. I believe our story can only be told when we feel we have the support, confidence and the courage to do so. Otherwise, we won't even try.

~Heather Mesaric

Regardless of the increasing numbers of physical and sexual child abuse cases being reported, I believe these figures do not reflect the actual totals. Violation of any magnitude occurs far more frequently than society can even begin to imagine. Those of us who were abused know how hard it is to disclose information about these incidences. Some never tell. I believe other victims like myself, will not share their secrets or let anyone into their world of silence until they feel safe enough to do so. With loss of trust, a major fallout from abuse, it's no wonder so much is left unsaid. Today's statistics simply do not reflect the true figures. *I was not counted*, were you?

The Justice Department of Canada defines child abuse as *"the violence, mistreatment or neglect that a child or adolescent may experience while in the care of someone they either trust or depend on, such as a parent, sibling, other relative, caregiver or guardian. Abuse may take place anywhere and may occur, for example, within the child's home or that of someone known to the child."* The government acknowledges, *"It has been difficult to obtain a complete picture of child abuse in Canada because it often remains hidden."* It also indicates that there are many different forms of child abuse and a child may be subjected to more than one form including: physical, sexual, photographic exploitation, neglect and emotional abuse to name a few. A 1998 study by The Canadian Incidence Study of Reported Child Abuse and Neglect (CIS) *"estimated that there were 135,573 child maltreatment investigations in Canada in 1998—a rate of almost 22 investigations for every 1000 children in Canada. Child welfare workers were able to confirm that the abuse had occurred in almost half (45%) of all cases."*

Health Canada's website states, *"Child sexual abuse occurs when a child is used for sexual purposes by an adult or adolescent. It involves exposing a child to any sexual activity or behaviour. Sexual abuse most often involves fondling and may include inviting a child to touch or be touched sexually. Other forms of sexual abuse include sexual intercourse, juvenile prostitution and sexual exploitation through child pornography. Sexual abuse is inherently emotionally abusive and is often accompanied by other forms of mistreatment. It is a betrayal of trust and an abuse of power over the child."* Also, they confirm my own findings on the reporting and supporting of sexually abused children by saying, *"Research consistently reveals that, for reasons such as these, most child victims do not disclose their abuse. Even when they do, additional barriers may be encountered. For many of the same reasons that children do not report the abuse, their families may, in turn, not seek help. If the family does want help, they may still encounter difficulties finding the appropriate services."*

Abuse of any kind has enormous, lasting repercussions. The media has helped expose the ugly truth about abuse with articles in magazines, newspapers and films that attempt to reveal how deeply victims are affected physically, emotionally and spiritually. I believe, however, that society is still not aware of how much this tragedy impacts every aspect of the lives of the victims.

The consequences of my physical and sexual abuse continue to be both subtle and at times detrimental to my life. I have been overly cautious with my feelings. I have tended to be suspicious of other peoples' actions and lacked the ability to trust. Many of my relationships have been superficial to protect myself from getting too close and I usually questioned my ability to make decisions. These are only a few of the end results I experienced from the abuse. Everyone who has been a part of my life has had to deal with some of these ramifications. Together we struggled and dealt with the conflicts that I endured on a daily basis.

I believe it's time to break the silence. The world needs to know more about this horrible offence taking place in many homes every day of some children's lives. Awareness is the only way to stop the abuse and help the victim. Physical and sexual abuse continues to be one of the best kept secrets in most families. The silence cannot be broken if the victim does not feel safe or doesn't know anyone they feel they can trust with their revelations. Disclosure cannot occur if the victim is afraid they will be blamed, or fear that the family unit will be torn apart—causing guilt or hate by other family members, or worse, not being believed at all. This was the main reason it took me years to admit what had happened. I knew I wouldn't be believed.

I feel strongly that it's everyone's responsibility to make this world a safer place for our children and to reveal the seriousness of abuse. I know it can start with me. I feel that if I break my silence it will encourage other victims to do the same. I want a chain reaction to result, so that the effects of physical and sexual abuse will be minimized for the victims and they can lead more fulfilling lives. The only way any of us can heal from abuse is to ***break our silence.***

To be successful with my healing process, I knew I needed to feel protected. In order for me to survive the abuse, I had pretended it didn't happen. When it was over, I hid the truth from the community I moved around in and especially the people closest to me. I acted as if nothing was wrong. This seemed to be the only logical solution. Nothing else made sense. Deep down, I knew the truth was that I had indeed been abused. I also knew my trials needed to be spoken out loud, but I wasn't sure anyone would listen to me or others in my position. I didn't know how to tell the authorities so that they would hear and understand my story.

In my opinion, society lacks sufficient support systems and organizations to deal with the healing process for victims of abuse. There are not enough groups, trained professionals or funds available to sustain support for all the casualties of these tragic circumstances. As well, I believe there is inadequate written material to help the victims understand the emotional roller coaster they are experiencing. Victims need to know they are not alone and have access to support so that they can come forward without fear of retribution or shame.

For these reasons, I felt I needed to write this book. The focus is on women healing from sexual and physical abuse by men. However, I encourage all victims of any type of abuse to utilize the tools they find here to aid in their recovery. My goal is to share my journey and inspire others to speak up for themselves. I want them to reclaim and heal their past. I want them to find a new way to live their lives, after abuse.

Each of us has the power to change our lives and I feel it can be done through positive thinking and affirmations. We can change the negative thoughts we have about ourselves and learn to deal with the inner turmoil that we experience on an everyday basis. We can become more caring, loving, supportive and nurturing towards ourselves with a process I call, *SELF-LOVE*. I believe that if we choose to, we can make a difference.

This book outlines the processes I used to heal from my physical and sexual abuse. It shares with you the emotions I felt prior to and during my healing process. The book also provides you with many exercises I used to release the pain, anger, and resentment that were a substantial part of my life. These activities helped me explore and learn more of how I thought and felt about myself. As well, the exercises allowed me to accept and continually implement my daily affirmations, which at times seemed silly and unproductive. There were a lot of intervals when intense healing was taking place without my conscious knowledge. Please keep this in mind while you are completing the tasks and daily affirmations. I can assure you, they changed my life in so many positive ways. I offer my journey of recovery so that others can heal, learn to love themselves, be free of guilt and most of all unveil the truth of their own story.

$\mathcal{M}$y Story—The Beginning Of My Journey

We all have a story to tell. Some are good, some are bad and others can be horrific.

~Heather Mesaric

I was born into a family of four children with an older sister and brother and one younger brother. My parents separated when I was about 4 years old because my father was jailed for physically abusing me. I lived with my mother until I was 7 years old when the courts, stunningly, ordered me to live with my father. They did not think that my mother could control me or keep me "safe." I was not allowed to see my mother because my father forbid any contact with her. I have often asked myself, "What were the courts thinking?" I went from the frying pan to the fire, or more appropriately, the bottom of a volcano. I did not understand why this had happened to me.

As far back as I can remember my father physically abused me. He thought nothing of slapping my face or head when I did something wrong. He often threw butcher knives at me and once knocked me unconscious. I remained that way for nearly a week because he was afraid to take me to a hospital or a doctor. He didn't want the abuse to be discovered. I was thrown down stairways and whipped with a belt so often it was very hard to hide the welts and bruises on my body. My brother and I would cover for my father's actions and I blamed child's play and accidents for the marks. On one occasion when I did tell a teacher what happened, a social worker visited our home. I learned a very hard lesson when my father brutalized me the following weekend in retaliation. I learned that *I could not tell anyone* what was really going on at home, for my own safety.

My father's parents were very cruel and the lack of love and respect in their home spilled into mine. My grandmother told my grandfather to go to his daughters for sex when she didn't feel like it. One summer my uncle and grandfather sexually abused me during a two-week visit. On one occasion, my brother and I witnessed my 15-year-old uncle trying to molest our 7-year-old brother and at a separate time, another of my uncles tried to have intercourse with his own sister. My father was no better as he took nude pictures of his common-law wife and sold them to his friends.

When I turned 8 years old, my father started bringing home male friends and they became interested in me, sexually. I found myself having to perform sexual acts on them and they would give me money or gifts. Around the age of 9, I began meeting strangers on the streets and became a child prostitute. I decided it couldn't be any worse than what was going on at home, where my father was constantly threatening my life. He almost killed me many times, as well as, letting the sexual abuse take place under everyone's noses. Living this nightmare was the foundation of "my secret" life. No one knew what was going on and they didn't seem to care. I felt I had no one to turn to for help.

When I was 11 years old, I was taken from my dad by the Children's Aid Society because of my "out of control behaviour" (stealing, truancy, staying out late, running away from home to name a few). The next time, I saw my father's family was at my grandmother's funeral twenty years later. I did have a few quick visits with my father in my early twenties. He moved into a nursing home after suffering a stroke and died when I was 38 years old.

After the Children's Aid Society stepped in, I stayed in a Receiving Centre for one year and a Treatment Home for another year. During this time, I learned that I was a great kid and that I could do anything I put my mind to. I learned to feel "safe" for the first time in my life. I was finally happy, learning to trust the adults around me, and creating dreams and goals. It was a new way for me to look at life. I thought I was going to be someone really special, even important.

At 13 years old, I was placed in a foster home. It was such a relief to have a "real family" to live with. I believed I could finally put my past to rest and live a so-called "normal life." Sadly, it turned out to be the beginning of a new round of abusive situations. Shortly after my arrival, my foster father began persistently touching, kissing and fondling me in sexual ways. He called it my "lessons on how to behave like a woman for my future boyfriends/husband." These "lessons" left me feeling, once again, dirty, ashamed and scared of what would happen next. I kept his actions a secret because I was afraid no one would believe me. I felt they would accuse me of lying. He and I always knew it was my word against his, and he would be believed before me. He was highly respected in his home, community and workplace. I, on the other hand, was a teenager placed with his family as a foster child because my parents were alcoholics unable to supervise me. It seemed he had his reputation to protect him and I had my past to discredit me. I was thought of as the troubled teen, without any hope or direction. Little did they know what the truth really was. During these adolescent years, I never told anyone, not even my best friends what was taking place behind closed doors. I couldn't take the chance that they would say something to their parents and I'd end up being thrown out and having to live on the streets.

My opportunity for a "normal life" was gone again and the old patterns of believing I was damaged goods surfaced. I no longer felt special or that I would ever be loved or wanted. I felt I was branded and became very promiscuous. This of course attracted guys who only wanted one thing – sex. These relationships further destroyed my already low self-esteem.

I believe being a victim means that you've experienced a situation against your will, a terrifying ordeal you do not have any control over. Those of us who have been victims understand the feelings of dread and helplessness when we suspect something is going to happen that we have no way of preventing. There was a time when I thought I must have been wearing a sign that read, "I am a victim (or easy). Do whatever you want to my body because I do not care what happens to me." Losing all hope, I believed I would always have struggles with men because I didn't deserve to be treated with dignity and respect. I thought I'd always be a *victim*.

Observing people around me, I knew I did not perceive the world as others did. I only saw hostility, crudeness, suspicion and sexual predators looking for power and control. Everything seemed so *confusing*. I was constantly confronted with self-doubt as to whether I was right or wrong, good or bad or had any talent other than sex to offer anyone.

I needed to find an escape and slowly created a "fantasy" world in my mind. The real one was too overwhelming for me and I could not remain a part of it all the time. I needed to imagine a place in my mind that I could go to when I was scared or didn't want to be a part of reality. I wanted a place that was mine, where no one could hurt me ever again. I invented a fictional world that kept me from seeing the truth of being abused.

I visited that special place often. It got to the point where I had a hard time separating fact from fantasy. Sometimes, I was not sure where one began and the other left off. They seemed to be intertwined. I did not realize that I was developing in my head life situations that were full of deception and distortion of what was real. I was in a world of my own, where I believed I had complete control over my life. This coping mechanism was just an exaggeration of my fictitious world.

At times, I would forget a lot of things I told people. I sometimes felt I had a split personality. I'd become upset when people relayed information to me that I didn't remember telling them, especially if it was anything personal. I would think to myself, "I couldn't have told them that!" I denied what they were saying, stating emphatically that they must have misunderstood what I said. Or I'd simply say they were thinking of someone else. Other times I would say nothing out of panic or embarrassment. In these situations, I wanted to run and hide. I avoided being around people for fear that they would learn more about my life and I'd scare them off. I thought they might think that I was a social outcast or trying to seek attention. These anxious episodes usually left me *remembering* things I wanted to forget. Old insecurities were intensified and I felt I was unable to handle my past or be honest about the abuse.

The abuse had left me with feelings of shame, disgust, uncertainty and fear. I knew something had to give. I wanted to have an ordinary life in which I could be proud that I was a survivor and not a victim. I was not sure how to make this happen; so, for a time, I convinced myself to pretend things were fine and hide the truth about the abuse.

In my late teens, the Children's Aid Society wanted to extend my position as a "ward of the crown" so that my continuing education would be paid for. This was out of the ordinary but they saw both my potential and my earnest desire to get a post-secondary degree. As part of the arrangements, I agreed to, I was reunited with my mother and sister on my 18th birthday. We would stay in touch from that point on. When I moved out of my foster home halfway through college, my foster father brought his daughters to visit me. He attempted to fondle me and it was then that I took a stand, ending over a decade of sexual abuse at the hands of many men who were responsible for my care and upbringing. Abuse would continue in my life because I still hadn't learned that I had the power to change how I was treated. While this was a significant turning point for me, it did not signal the end of the emotional suffering.

In my last year of college, I met a wonderful man who was finishing his university degree. He came from a very loving and caring family with a strong sense of togetherness. I was welcomed into their home and became a cherished family member when we married. However, my anxieties and lack of sexual desire prevented my husband and I from having a normal relationship. I was afraid of intimacy and did not allow him to get too close for fear I would have to deal with the abuse.

Then, everything changed, when after four years of marriage, I became pregnant. Suddenly, I could no longer pretend I was okay and that the abuse of the past had no bearing on my present life. I began questioning my ability to be a good mother and kept praying that the child would be a boy. I did not want a girl. I was afraid that if I had a daughter she would be sexually abused by someone and I'd be powerless to stop it, as I'd been with myself. I thought that if I had a boy, I would not have to deal with this topic ever again. I wanted to forget the abuse had happened and go on with my life.

When the doctor told me I had a baby girl, I was devastated. It was the opening of wounds I'd tried to bury and brought to life my greatest worries. It quickly became very clear to me just how much of my past had not been resolved.

Having never been properly taken care of as a child, I realized how unprepared I was to be a mother. I feared I would never be a good parent since I had no experience of a loving and nurturing mother.

The new baby offered one more excuse for fights between my husband and I. My fears of being a poor wife and mother intensified. As a parent, I became very over-protective and guarded our child like a watchdog. When I was not with her, I had panic attacks. It was hell! My fears ran wild, and in my mind, I questioned every move my husband made towards our daughter. I did not want him to change or bathe her. When he spent time with her, I worried constantly, especially if I was not in the same room or was out of the house. I made sure this rarely happened by taking her with me or having him do our errands. In an effort to protect her as I had never been, I hardly ever left her side. Sleeping very lightly, I would stand and listen at the doorway if I heard my husband get up in the night. It was a way of being sure he was not going to her room. *I had absolutely no reason to believe my husband would ever harm our daughter* but *I was wary of any male who took an interest in her.*

Family gatherings became a nightmare for me. My husband's parents, brothers, sisters, and their families were all so kind, yet I couldn't control my unfounded suspicions. I constantly watched everyone and prevented them from holding my daughter for too long. If she was out of my view for more than a few minutes, I became frantic and annoyed. I was a women possessed with incestuous thoughts and every male became guilty in my eyes. Given the right situation, I believed they were all capable of committing indecent acts. I was not about to make it possible with my daughter. My fears were directly linked to my past, and therefore, I did not believe there were men who would never abuse a child under any circumstances.

There were times when I felt like a human radar detector, constantly tuning in for the worst. I tried so hard to glimpse beauty in the world, yet all I saw was fear, anger and doubt. It didn't seem to me that a man and a child could have a positive and loving relationship without it being sexual. When I saw children with a male adult, I automatically wondered if the child was all right or being molested. Seeing a man give a child a hug or kiss, my thoughts would race back to the years of my abuse I'd been desperately trying to forget. I felt like I was on a merry-go-round, always going in circles, never moving ahead and not knowing how to stop this cycle for good.

Whenever I thought about my past, I became **enraged**. The **anger** resulted from knowing I had lost my childhood and adolescence. Since I'd never learned how to form meaningful adult relationships, I was not able to give or receive affection in a loving and caring manner. I continuously doubted my worthiness and held a very low opinion of myself. I didn't think I deserved to be loved, believing instead that I was just a sex object with nothing special to offer anyone.

The internal rage persisted and while I wanted to deal with it, it frightened me. I felt that if I ever really released my anger I'd go crazy and try to hurt the person(s) who wounded me. I was afraid that I would seek revenge for their ruination of my life. I wanted them to suffer as I had suffered all these years. More menacing to me was the thought that releasing the pent-up anger might trigger a nervous breakdown and I might completely lose control of all of my emotions.

I was more afraid of my anger and my desire for revenge, than I was of the sexual abuse. The abuse itself had always come to an end. It had never lasted more than an hour at a time and I doubted my anger could be so easily contained. I just didn't know if once ignited, it would ever stop, even if I expressed all the pain I was feeling inside.

When I displayed my temper, it was always out of context and out of control. I was constantly angry over little things and rarely expressed myself appropriately. Screaming and shouting at everyone over unimportant things, I took my anger out on the people I cared about. When I was in a rage, I hated the world around me and myself. Although I wanted desperately to act and feel normal, I had no idea how to change. I wanted to stop these outbursts and handle situations with less ferocity. While I wanted everything to calm down, I could not be certain that everything would be fine. I did not know how to trust others or myself.

Trusting was very difficult for me because I'd been betrayed by my caregivers so many times. People I relied on had harmed me and made me do things that did not feel right. I'd learned that sometimes adults continue to do hurtful things when you ask them to stop and then seem unconcerned about the consequences of their actions. To me, children were powerless and it was better not to question what was right or wrong.

Even trusting myself was lost when the adults around me dismissed my instincts. With no self-confidence, I disbelieved my own thoughts and feelings.

My lack of trust was problematic for all my relationships. If someone told me they loved me, I could not and did not believe them. I would say to myself, "Sure you do. I can fulfill your sexual needs, why would you not love me?" It never occurred to me that someone could love me for who I was. I never let my defences down and I stopped everyone from developing an intimate relationship with me.

On a deeper level, I felt that I was to **blame** for the abuse. I constantly sabotaged my relationships in order to somehow punish myself. Logically, I knew I was not at fault, however, in the back of my mind, I keep playing games that said just maybe I had caused the abuse or asked for it.

It was hard for me to let go of my critical attitude. I was always on guard and was very dissatisfied with people in my life, especially men. I believed that they had to be perfect in order to make up for all the other "jerks" in my life. I also seemed to find fault in everything the men in my relationships did in order to cover up all my deficiencies. I felt that criticizing them would make me feel better about myself. However, the more I focused on what I perceived as their shortcomings, the more I drove myself crazy thinking that they didn't live up to my standards. This helped me keep a safe distance between us.

Family life was difficult. I did not know what a family was supposed to be like. I only knew what I'd been shown in the past which was distorted and dysfunctional. The dictionary states that dysfunctional is "impaired or abnormal functioning." This certainly describes the family life that I experienced with my real parents and my foster family.

When our first child was two years old, our second daughter was born. I experienced the same feelings and emotions that were brought on by the first birth. Now, I knew I had to find a way to heal. I had to find the strength to believe that I was a mother who could provide safety, warmth, and most of all, love. I came to the realization that I could not do this without first loving and accepting myself for who I was. I had to uncover a solution that would enable me to put my past to rest and learn to live in the here and now. It was time to learn to be happy and content with my life.

Deciding that I wanted my life back meant dealing with the abuse head on. I saw it as the only way to move forward in my life and especially in my role as a mother. I'd lost my dignity, my trust in others, my childhood, my self-worth and so much more. It was time to reclaim my life.

Some days the task felt impossible and I had no answers to my questions. I found myself puzzling, where do I go for help? What is this healing process all about? What will it feel like to be healed? How will I know if I am really healing from the abuse? What will I ask for when I find the resources? What should I deal with first: the abuse, my anger or present day behaviours? There seemed to be so many questions and very few answers. I had no idea what to do next and most of all, I didn't know who I could trust.

If any of the above sounds familiar... believe me, you're not alone. I kept telling myself, there is hope. I can be in control of my life in a positive way. The future starts today, right now. My life changed when I decided to change it. Let me share my healing process with you.

*M*y Healing Process

Sometimes we have to step out of our comfort zone in order to discover new perceptions that validate new awareneses of ourselves. One step at a time – baby steps will be just fine – as long as we get to where we need to go.

~Heather Mesaric

I knew my healing journey would be painful and at times scary. If I did nothing, I'd be a victim for the rest of my life, something I definitely did not want. Because I had survived sexual abuse, I knew I had tremendous strengths that I could use to help me heal. That is very important for every survivor to know. There was a little voice inside me saying, "Use this strength, you can heal." I heard the message that the rewards would be well worth the struggle, and my life would finally be mine to cherish. I started out by listening to these small whispers and over time, I learned to love the world around me and myself. For once, I trusted my instincts and most of all I embraced my choices and decisions.

Forcing myself to reach out and ask for help from others was essential. At times during my healing process my support system was my life line. It consisted of my second husband, my sister, friends, and therapists. Without them, I truly do not know where I would be today. Together we faced my emotions and insecurities during my recovery.

There are a variety of methods that can be used to aid in healing. We all have individual needs, strengths and motivation levels, which could affect the outcome of our healing process. I believe we take our own personal journey of recovery because we have different life experiences and expectations. Each person has their own blueprint to start with and can make changes as they pass through every day life experiences and empowering little miracles. In other words, we make our path in life depending on how we interpret or act upon each situation we encounter.

My only limitation during my journey of healing was my imagination. Therefore, I kept an open mind and I gave myself permission to experience all the emotions that surfaced. I allowed myself the opportunity to find the real me and eventually the happiness I deserved. I needed to work at my own pace and could not rush it. I understood the process would entail many stages and struggles, depending on my ability to deal with what was happening at any given time. I allowed myself to be my own guide and to trust my inner voice. I kept a journal of my feelings, thoughts and ongoing progress. As well, I made myself complete the exercises that are included in this book, in order to take a deeper look at what I was experiencing during specific periods of time.

Occasionally, it was extremely painful and difficult. Even while writing this book, I wanted to pretend the abuse happened to someone else and not me. However, you can be certain I am talking about my life. At some point, I faced and felt every emotion and situation that is published in this book. The healing process requires you to go through many stages and I did not heal over-night. I believe it's a life-long transformation and it takes time to discover the wonderful you.

$\mathcal{P}$ointers On How To Use This Book

The book is divided into five major sections: ***Primary Healing, Secondary Healing, Personal Healing, Enlightenment Healing and Lifetime Healing.***

There are several components in each of the five major sections. I call these, healing units. The units are self-explanatory with a description of my feelings and examples of how each unit has affected my life.

Exercises have been included in each unit to assist your healing process. These were powerful tools I used to make life-changing decisions and you may wish to complete them, as well. If you choose to do them, you will need a lined notebook. I refer to my notebook as a *"journal."* These exercises I call *"journal assignments"* and may provoke feelings you have blocked from memory. Often after completing my assignments, I needed to share my reactions with my support group. Sometimes I felt sadness, anger and disappointment and other times relief, joy and even excitement. Most of all, the work helped me to understand why I was thinking and behaving in particular ways.

If you choose to complete the exercises, I highly stress the importance of creating your own support system. I believe being heard by a compassionate listener is vital to recovery. This person/persons may be a close friend, family member, marital partner or therapist. If you do not have someone you feel you can trust, ask your family doctor or contact a local help line for a referral to a professional. As well, you may refer to the back of book on page 266 - Resources for Phone Numbers or Websites, in order to assist you if you do not know where to seek help in your local area. Specifically look for a recognized agency dealing with abuse, an organization with accredited practitioners on staff or an individual with a connection to large treatment facilities. You will find this a valuable asset as you begin to unravel feelings and emotions you once controlled with suppression.

Releasing buried feelings is necessary for healing to take place. Having someone witness these expressions of emotion can be very therapeutic. I found that when I shared these feelings with someone face to face, I could then vent my anger into my journal writings in a more focused manner. It was a great comfort to have someone hold me when I cried. I learned it was not only okay to shed tears or be angry but that it actually helped me get rid of the weight I'd been carrying. Holding on to the pain keeps us stuck in the past. Trust yourself and let go. Listen to your inner guidance to know when the time is right for you. Be kind to yourself and use your support system. If you find that at some point they are not helping, look for someone else. There is always help if you are willing to let people into your life to encourage you through the long nights/days that you may face.

Throughout the book, in each healing unit I have provided *"Affirmations."* Affirmations are powerful statements we make that declare how we want our lives to be, how we want ourselves to feel and how we want to see the world. Repeated on a daily basis or as often as you need them, it is a form of re-training your negative thought patterns into positives. Using affirmations can, and will, change your life if you incorporate them into your routine. The more I re-programmed my self-defeating internal dialogue, the better I felt about the changes I was making and about myself. I wanted my "self-fulfilling prophecy" to be a positive one. I wanted to like who I was and to learn to love myself completely.

Parker Palmer is quoted as saying, *"No punishment anyone might inflict on us could possibly be worse than the punishment we inflict on ourselves by conspiring in our own diminishment."* Stopping the flow of hurtful talk is a challenge that can be met with success when you use affirmations. *Remember* whether you know it now or not, you *are* wonderful and you are entitled to be loved. You <u>are</u> special in every way, and don't you forget it!

Like any *new* habit, using affirmations takes practice. Over time, you will notice a change in your attitude towards yourself and those around you as you start to believe in what you are saying in your affirmations.

I knew that the more strongly I believed in these statements, the more I would benefit from them. I became happier in almost every aspect of my life while using the affirmations. I started to feel differently about who I was and began to see the world without the veil of darkness I'd been using. Rather than just pain, fear and suffering, I had a better understanding of what the world really had to offer me. My journal exercises and daily affirmations gave me the tools to love myself and others around me.

Please note: I personally found the exercises and affirmations in this book to be very beneficial which is why I am offering them to you. I cannot promise that they will work in the same way for you, but what I do know is that they provide an excellent starting point to begin your journey. You may want to modify some of the work to make it suit your specific needs. As individuals, we bring different strengths and weaknesses to our healing process. I do believe that if you give them a try, you may find valuable tools in these assignments.

Primary Healing

*H*ow To Use The
"Primary Healing" Section

I strongly recommend you read and complete the exercises and affirmations in this section first. They are the ones I use in my workshops and healing weekend seminars. The work in the Primary Healing Section was the foundation that was essential for me to begin my healing process. I needed to look deep inside, explore my fears, anger, and other emotions before further healing could take place.

In relating my story I intentionally **bolded,** some words that were very significant to my healing process. They are: Victim, Confusing, Remembering, Enraged/Anger, Trust and Blame. The feelings associated with these words had to be dealt with for my healing to begin. I have examined them in detail and they appear in sub-units throughout the Primary Healing Section.

I suggest you read and work through the "Primary Healing Section" slowly. It touches the heart of the emotions surrounding abuse and needs a lot of attention. Have patience and be gentle with yourself while doing the exercises and affirmations.

The units are in the order that I felt worked best for me. I strongly believe I needed to complete each unit in the precise order given for me to progress to the next step of recovery.

You may find that certain units spark more awareness of forgotten memories and/or feelings than others. As well, they may stir up hidden fears. I noticed that as I healed, I became more conscious of incidents from the past and had to deal with my feelings regarding these situations. This could happen with you, so please do not be alarmed. You may find yourself reacting as you did when the abuse first took place. Ask for comfort from your support group and allow yourself to get in touch with your lost inner child. You may notice that certain feelings continue to surface repeatedly. If this happens, do not get discouraged or anxious. It just means that in this case, the pain runs a little deeper. Write about your thoughts and try to discover why this is happening and what is still waiting to be resolved. In order for me to let go of my anger, I needed to do some of my exercises numerous times to release everything I had brewing inside. I had so much hate, hostility and resentment that I had to work at different stages throughout my healing. You too, may need to repeat some exercises more than once in order to benefit and feel you can fully move ahead. Allow yourself the opportunity to get in touch with whatever you are feeling.

I suggest the affirmations be used as often as possible during the day to get the maximum benefit from them. Write them down; put them in your purse or wallet, on the dashboard of your car, on your desk at work, on the refrigerator or anywhere highly visible. I wrote mine on a small index card and carried it everywhere, reading them often. The car was the perfect place for me because I was stuck in traffic at least fifteen minutes, three or four times a day. This gave me the opportunity to frequently reinforce my positive statements with no inconvenience.

Each day I gave myself a new affirmation. The affirmations were very short, easy to say and remember. I said them in the order given in each of the Healing Units. Remember, these are what worked for me and you can change the order or specific words to maximize their effect for you. Your affirmations must be stated in a positive manner; example; "I will do_____" or "I can do _____." Avoid making statements with a negative tone such as: "I will not be fat." Instead, say, "I will become healthy." "I will not be angry," could become "I will find new ways to deal with my anger." When we use the negative statement, our brain focuses on resistance, creating more self-destructive situations like those that caused the problem in the first place. With the example of "I will not be fat," the mind will hone in on the word "fat" and want to manifest fat in your life. If you say, "I will become healthy," the mind directs its energy towards the word "healthy" and seeks healthy living. The same goes with anger. The mind will find things to make you angry unless you make the statement, "I will find new ways to deal with my anger." This positive statement prompts the mind to be open to new possibilities.

Tears

I cry silently in the night,
I cry when no one can hear me,
I cry for my pain,
I cry for the shame,
I cry for the loneliness I feel,
I cry when there seems to be no hope in sight,
I cry to release my anger,
I cry when I feel out of control,
I cry when no one listens,
I cry because I do not know what else to do,
I cry because I feel like a child in an adult body,
I cry because it makes me feel better,
I cry because it is the right thing to do,
I cry for the sake of crying.

It's okay to cry, for whatever the reason!

—Heather Mesaric

*S*uicidal Thoughts and A Contract

When we cannot keep ourselves safe from ourselves we need to entrust others to do the job for us.

~Heather Mesaric

There were many times when I was a teenager that I felt I wanted to end my life. I honestly believed I did not have anything to live for. Hours at a time, I would think about how and when I would kill myself. It seemed like the only solution I had to rid myself of the pain I was feeling from the abuse. On my 17th birthday I was hospitalized from an overdose of aspirins. I swallowed an entire bottle, hoping to end my life. Luckily, I panicked and told someone what I'd done. For a long time afterwards, I carried the fear that I would harm myself again. I did not trust that I would be able to take care of myself.

There were times I would inflict pain on my body or bite my fingernails until they bled. Somehow this made me feel better. I know there are many people who cut or hurt themselves in order to release the emotions they are feeling. *I cannot stress enough that you need to seek professional help with these self-abusive tendencies.* Believe me when I say that you deserve the best for yourself. While I feel getting competent professional assistance is some of the best advice I can offer you, I believe that if you do not want to seek qualified help at this time, then *you must confide in a support team.*

It is so important that you share this information with someone who is willing to help you with these dark feelings. You need someone who is prepared to be available twenty-four hours a day to help you manage these thoughts.

Most major cities and small towns have a 24-hour HELP-LINE or Crisis Line service. You don't have to give your name or address and they can assist you with finding organizations that deal with survivors of sexual or physical abuse. You can also speak to your doctor or religious leader about a referral to a good professional who will assist you in your thoughts of suicide and or hurting yourself.

My first therapist made me write a contract with her. Basically, it stated that I would call her when I was feeling suicidal. Also, I agreed that I would call a friend and either visit or talk on the phone with them if I was feeling suicidal, depressed, vulnerable, scared or lonely.

Writing the contract really helped me to think about the options I had besides taking my life. (I did not want to die. I just wanted the pain to go away.) We called the contract, "MY LIFE CONTRACT." I wrote, "I will call either my therapist or someone on my support team when I am feeling suicidal. I will not harm myself in anyway. I promise to make verbal and physical contact with someone as soon as I get these feelings. If I am unable to get in touch with someone, I will call the help-line and talk to the person who answers the phone."

After signing the contract I posted it where I could see it at all times. I did have these feelings and had to make calls to my therapist and friends during my healing process. This contract really was a life-saver for me because it kept the destructive thoughts as just thoughts and not actions. I did not want to break the contract and respected the commitment my therapist had made by being my emergency contact. As I healed, I no longer had thoughts of hurting myself.

You will need to make this agreement with someone you can trust with the knowledge that you sometimes have these urges. Making this pledge may be difficult for some of you and for others it may be a welcome relief. Knowing that you have someone in place who is vowing to share with you and listen is vital. You must be totally honest with them about your plans to hurt or kill yourself. You need to describe any past experiences of self-abuse or attempts on your life. This will help them understand and guide them into what steps to take for you, whether it's to call the hospital, your doctor, or your therapist. They need this information to help you face these situations more appropriately.

If you have suicidal thoughts or if you have hurt yourself in the past, please seriously consider writing a "Life Contract" with someone. The act of putting your commitment to life on paper is a way to make it real for you.

Journal Assignment: Write in your journal, (lined notebook), "I will not follow through with any plans to hurt/kill myself. Instead, I will call my contact person." Write your contact person(s) names and phone numbers by the phone and keep it there in case you need it. You may want to write up your own contract using your own words that will assist you in making that call when you have these urges. You will need a contract that you can enforce when you are out of control or when you are not thinking in a healthy manner. Write it so you will be able to make the contact that is needed in order to save your life.

Journal Assignment – Exercise Two: Write down 3 to 5 things you <u>want to **live for**</u>. **Yes**, this is hard, it took me a long, long time to think of things that were positive about my life, yet, I did come up with a few. One of my primary reasons was for my children and family. I knew they depended on me and I didn't want to hurt them in anyway. Think about this for awhile and come up with your own reasons for wanting to live. **Please note**: do this exercise on a <u>good</u> day - don't try to do this, if you are feeling angry, lonely, scared or if you are feeling any other negative emotion. This exercise would not be very productive for you to complete during any of these vulnerable times. The exercise must be done when you are in a positive and healthy state of mind, so that you can think *positively and openly* about the benefits of staying alive.

Your Weeks Affirmations: These are the ones that I used and found very helpful. For the next week say the following affirmations as often as possible, in order to create new patterns of "positive thinking." Some days I repeated them more than ten times in an hour or whenever I thought about them. My index cards really helped me to keep saying them often. Remember, you can create your own if these do not say what is in your heart.

Day one: I commit to making myself safe.
Day two: I am seeking the help I need to make myself safe.
Day three: I follow through with my commitment to make myself safe.
Day four: I have created a safe environment for myself.
Day five: I am a loving and nurturing person; I am gentle and loving with myself
Day six: I am making myself safe in every way. I love who I am.
Day seven: I am able to seek or call for help if I need to. I love myself.

Remember: You are not alone in this process. Seek the support you need to heal from the trauma of sexual abuse. There are people who truly want to help you. You need to let them help and assist you. Talk to a professional who understands how you are feeling and someone who can help you get these self-abusive inclinations under control.

On the next page is a sample of a "Life Contact" to use as a guideline and may be photocopied.

My Life Contract

I agree not to hurt myself in any way and when I get feelings of wanting to hurt myself, I agree to contact the following person immediately.

I _____ will call my emergency contact person _____ at phone number _____ to let them know that I am having feelings of hurting myself.

If _____ is not available, I agree to call my emergency backup person or agency _____ at phone number _____.

I agree to let them know my plans and if I have to go to the hospital for assistance I agree to let them help me.

Date: _____

Signatures:
Myself: _____
My Contact Person: _____
Alternate Contact/Agency: _____

Author Heather Mesaric gives permission to photocopy this page from her book: It's Time To H.E.A.L. (ISBN 1-4120-6247-0 – Trafford Publishing at Trafford.com/05-1148)

*B*eing A Victim

When we think of ourselves as victims we give away our power. We surrender to the belief that we have no control over how we can handle situations. You may have been a victim, but you are a survivor as well.

~Heather Mesaric

The Encarta World Dictionary defines a victim as "*a) somebody or something harmed by an act or circumstance; b) somebody who is tricked or taken advantage of; and c) somebody who experiences misfortune and feels helpless to do anything about it.*" It was an important step for me to admit that while I had been victimized, I had also allowed myself to be a victim. I had to realize that I could take back control of my life and begin making good decisions for myself. I knew there would be times when I might be skeptical and on guard around other people and that was okay because, *it was my choice*. I kept saying to myself, "***I am not going to be a victim ever again***."

I wanted to stop the pattern of victim thinking. It was in my power to change the way things were happening to me and I started believing I could do it. More importantly, I began believing in myself.

This step was very hard for me because I knew it was critical to my recovery and failure seemed a strong possibility. I'd had so many setbacks. To make changes, I had to have faith in myself and in what I was doing. Up to this point in my life, I had constantly put myself down. Now, I began asking myself to change this habit and think positive thoughts about my abilities and who I could be. While at first it was not that simple, I kept telling myself, "Get through this and you'll be well on your way to making a better life for yourself."

As I practiced my affirmations I learned being positive was much less work than I thought. I told myself, "I deserve a better life. I deserve happiness. I deserve much more." I knew I had to change how I felt about myself and that meant believing I could make the necessary changes. One way was using these powerful declarations of self-worth; so, I repeated to myself, "I am a wonderful person." I said it every chance I got during the day to get over the idea that what I was doing was foolish.

Journal Assignment—Exercise One: Over the next few days, write in your journal all the information that relates to your thinking of yourself as a victim. You can use short sentences or just words such as "at work," "in the grocery store," "talking to a friend," etc. The list can be as short or long as you want it to be. Take your time doing this exercise. Think about the different situations where you think you have been a victim. The purpose is for you to get in touch with the real meaning of the word "victim" for you. Explore your feelings on being a victim. Answer these questions to become more aware of those inner feelings that are locked deep inside you: *What does being a victim mean to you?* and *How do you see yourself as a victim?*

Journal Assignment—Exercise Two: When this list has been done to your satisfaction do the following: re-read the lists slowly and after each example say aloud, "I will no longer be a victim in this situation."

Please note: This process may take several tries until you begin to believe you are not a victim. It was very important for me to take this step extremely slow. I had to convince myself that this would help and overcome the feeling of how silly it seemed to be talking out loud to myself. Hearing the words is a profound way to bring meaning to the message.

Journal Assignment—Exercise Three: The next important step for me was to **admit and accept** that I really was in control of my life. I had to believe, "I was no longer going to be a victim." This meant acknowledging I had allowed myself to be a victim in some situations where I could have prevented it.

I constantly asked myself how I was feeling. I needed to get in touch with what was going on inside and how I was perceiving what was being said or done in my presence. My body signals told me when I was feeling victimized by a tightening in my stomach, perspiration and sometimes a strong inclination to burst into tears. Now I was learning that if I did not like what was happening, I could choose to ignore it, speak up or leave the situation. It was entirely up to me. For example, if someone cut in front of me in a check-out line or a clerk spoke rudely to me, I defended myself. When my husband accused me of not doing something he thought I should have, I responded as an adult and not as a frightened child. In most cases, I found myself exerting my newfound power by saying, "I didn't like that." For the first time, I told people how I felt about what they were doing to me. Some of the responses were simply, "Oh, I didn't know that bothered you. Sorry." What a power trip for me. It gave me the courage to keep persevering. It also allowed me to make healthier choices about whom I wanted to associate with. I could say "no" to people or just avoid them altogether. Distancing myself from people who hurt my feelings and situations that made me feel uncomfortable became routine. I started taking control of my life.

At this stage, I want you to continuously say to yourself, *"I am not a victim. I am not a victim."* Again, I stress; you must believe this.

You can stop the cycle of victimization. It is in your power if you believe in yourself. Sometimes the hardest step is the first one, however, it will get easier, especially when you believe in your own abilities. You are a wonderful person and you deserve to be happy. When the times get tough, remember; these methods have worked for me or this book would not be in print today.

Your Weeks Affirmations: These are the ones that I used and found very helpful. For the next week say the following affirmations as often as possible, in order to create new patterns of "positive thinking." Some days I repeated them more than ten times in an hour or whenever I thought about them. My index cards really helped me to keep saying them often. Remember, you can create your own if these do not say what is in your heart.

Day one: I am a survivor. I am a survivor.
Day two: I am protecting myself in a healthy way.
Day three: I have many choices in life. I am a survivor.
Day four: I am now making choices that are good for me.
Day five: I am making choices that will improve my total well-being.
Day six: I love the choices that I am making for myself.
Day seven: I make loving, caring and supportive choices for myself.

Journal Assignment—Exercise Four: When you have completed the above week of affirmations, make another list of the times during the last week only, when you feel you have been a victim, if at all.

Journal Assignment—Exercise Five: Write in your journal in very large print, "**I am a survivor**. I have choices. I make wise decisions. I love who I am and I am wonderful." Write these phrases as many times as it takes until you fully grasp what they mean to you. Read these often to fortify the positive messages that you are saying to yourself.

Your Weeks Affirmations: These affirmations are the same as the ones completed in exercise three. They are needed to reinforce the belief that you no longer need to be a victim and that you are a survivor. I suggest you complete these affirmations again for another week.

Day one: I am a survivor. I am a survivor.
Day two: I am protecting myself in a healthy way.
Day three: I have many choices in life. I am a survivor.
Day four: I am now making choices that are good for me.
Day five: I am making choices that will improve my total well-being.
Day six: I love the choices that I am making for myself.
Day seven: I make loving, caring and supportive choices for myself.

You may find that you are becoming more aware of people who do things that put you in an uncomfortable position. You can change this. After doing my journal assignments, I found I was looking at these situations differently. I discovered that I was letting people put me down or that they were doing things I did not like or agree with. Afraid to stand up for myself or of being hurt, I was allowing them to do these things. I was also fearful that I would not be liked if I disagreed or told them to stop. There were a hundred reasons why I was frightened and continued allowing myself to be a victim. I didn't believe I deserved anything better and my biggest hurdle was, again, to stop seeing myself as a victim.

Continue to say the above affirmations until you honestly feel that you are not thinking of yourself as a victim. It has been said many times, and I know it is the truth, that no one can make you do anything you do not wish to do. You do indeed have choices. You can decide what is best for you and enjoy the new freedom you have given yourself by relinquishing your status as a victim. Be proud, stand tall and love yourself. You have so much to offer yourself and others.

My journal work helped me to realize that I had the ability to make changes. The progress was slow and there were times I thought I could not overcome my victim mentality. I knew eventually I would get better at preventing or changing my behaviours and ultimately heal this area of my life. Learning to recognize when I did not react the way I wanted to, was the key to changing this old pattern.

Remember: This process takes time and each day will be a new and different day for you. What you do not get done today will wait for tomorrow. Pat yourself on the back for all the hard work and the progress you have made. Be proud of yourself. Give yourself a big hug. You deserve it.

*C*onfusion

If I have no guidelines or positive examples to follow, then how can I truly know what is right or wrong and how can I possibly make choices for myself, if I don't know they are mine to make.

~*Heather Mesaric*

During the next stage of my journey, I explored my feelings of confusion. This included both my past and present thoughts about what had happened and what I could do to understand it all.

At the time, I was very confused about my role as a partner and wife. Having no adequate role models, I did not know how to act. Conflicting thoughts kept flooding in and during these times, I would have to remind myself that it was okay for my husband to touch me in a sexual way. I struggled with convincing myself he was touching me out of love. I would get tense and afraid. I'd push him away or start a fight to keep my distance from him. I could not separate my past from my present day and did not know how to tell him what I was feeling.

There were others times when everyday situations were so overwhelming for me. The very thought of making a decision, seemed too much effort. These were basic choices like, "Should I get out of bed today?" or "Should I get dressed or stay in my nightgown?" or "Should I do the chores around the house?" It would take me hours to figure out what I should do and some days I ended up doing nothing at all. If at all possible, I avoided making decisions. When friends or family asked,

"What do you want to do?" I'd reply, "Oh anything, it's up to you." What they did not know was that I could not make up my mind and was often incapable of thinking things through. I could not form clear thoughts or keep the thoughts that I did have straight. My attention seemed scattered and unorganized. I had trouble remembering from one moment to the next and could not keep past sexual encounters separate from my every day life. Everything was meshed together.

Initially I had to allow myself to do nothing and not feel guilty about it. I had always felt I had to be super-woman, super-mom, or super-employee. A big test was giving myself permission to be a mess instead. I needed to let myself stop worrying about getting everything done and being perfect. I had to convince myself it was okay to set things aside for another time and be content with having things just "be." In reality, I knew I would not likely get anything done in this state anyway, so I took a little break from the world. Several times, I called in sick, stayed in bed and spent the time alone crying and sleeping.

This is when I discovered that I'd been hiding from the truth by keeping myself on a chaotic roller coaster. Subconsciously, I was staying occupied by fulfilling all my imagined responsibilities to avoid dealing with the facts. Keeping busy was a way to have no time to think about my life or my past. It was in a sense how I ran from the abuse.

Seeing this, I knew I needed to "slow down" and stop racing in so many activity-laden directions. Eliminating the congestion in my life would definitely help to sharpen my focus.

Ironically, my confusion really stemmed from doing too much. In order to keep myself on track I started writing things down and setting goals. I made lists and forced myself to follow them with an aim to complete one task at a time. Up until now, I would begin a project, get distracted and start another task. My house was filled with unfinished ventures. This included mundane jobs like laundry still in the dryer and dishes in water in the sink to more ambitious things like sewing material all over the floor.

Once I started writing things out and actually finishing what I'd started, I began to feel good. I may have only had one or two things on the list, but I was able to do them. I began feeling as though I could handle day-to-day routines. My biggest accomplishment was learning to organize my thoughts and my life in general. To this day, I still set goals and make lists for myself. I have a "TO DO LIST" for each day. Sometimes I get everything done on my list and other times I only do a couple of things. That's okay since I'm in control of the list and can revise it any time I choose to. I no longer beat myself up for not getting enough done. Now, I pat myself on the back for doing what I did, whether it's relaxing on the couch or cleaning the house. I've learned to be more forgiving of myself. Also, I know how to stay focused and organized each day by following my lists and goals.

This process was extremely challenging and at first I had a hard time sticking to a list. I felt drawn to my old habits of trying to do too many things, which always resulted in nothing being done. It took me a few attempts before I saw the benefit of structure. Ultimately, I was more productive, more organized, and I was handing in reports at work in a timely manner. What a joy that was for me.

My recommendation is that you have only one list. For a while, I started new lists on different occasions and ended up with lists all over the place. I resorted to making one list that I pinned on the refrigerator and kept it there. Now, when I feel the need to make a new list, I rip up the old one so there are no duplicates.

If you find yourself frequently feeling confused, this organizing of thoughts may be beneficial to you. My philosophy is to try everything and then you'll know what works best for you.

Journal Assignment: Over the next few days, make a list of all the things you need to remember or want to do during the day. Try to be realistic with your goals list. If you know you can only do one thing during the day, then only write one thing on the page. However, if you normally do a hundred and one things as I did, write down a few things and complete them. Remember to set yourself up to win and be sure to allow yourself some time to do nothing.

Journal Assignment—Exercise Two: When you have completed something on your list, cross it off. If you are ready, do the next thing on the list and stroke it off when it's done. If something comes up and you cannot do what you wanted to do, tell yourself it's okay. The task is still on the list for you to complete at another time. It works best if you try to stick to the list as much as possible until you establish a habit of finishing things. The goal here is to feel successful and be proud of your accomplishments.

Your Weeks Affirmations: These are the ones that I used and found very helpful. For the next week say the following affirmations as often as possible, in order to create new patterns of "positive thinking." Some days I repeated them more than ten times in an hour or whenever I thought about them. My index cards really helped me to keep saying them often. Remember, you can create your own if these do not say what is in your heart.

Day one: My future is full of possibilities for myself. I am safe.

Day two: I have control over what I can and cannot do.

Day three: I am focused for today. I like how I am improving in everything I do.

Day four: I now have feelings that are more loving and caring towards myself.

Day five: I have control over my life. I make good decisions for myself.

Day six: I am making great decisions in my life more and more everyday.

Day seven: I am making positive changes; I love how I feel about myself.

Remember: You have just given yourself a new tool to help you get organized. You have come a long way. Keep up the great effort. Be loving towards yourself and give yourself a big hug. Be proud of who you have become.

My TO DO List For Today

Date: _____

Things I Need or Want to Do Today   Complete

- _____ ☐
- _____ ☐
- _____ ☐
- _____ ☐
- _____ ☐
- _____ ☐
- _____ ☐
- _____ ☐
- _____ ☐
- _____ ☐

Appointments / Birthdays / Anniversary or Other Special Dates or Events To Remember…

- _____ ☐
- _____ ☐
- _____ ☐
- _____ ☐
- _____ ☐

Positive Statements I say To Myself To Help Me Stay Organized…

- _____ ☐
- _____ ☐
- _____ ☐
- _____ ☐
- _____ ☐

Why Can't I Remember

I know, I'm different than others my age,
I feel it when I am told, "You are weird".
I know, my behaviour is out of control at times,
I feel it when people walk away from me.
I know, there is a reason why I find it hard to trust,
I feel it through my tears and sorrow.
I know, something is wrong,
I feel it with every breath I take.
I know, my body is trying to speak to me,
I feel it when I shake and withdraw from the world.
I know, there are memories locked away for a reason,
I feel it in my fears.

I know, I am trying to run from something,
I am just not sure from what or why.
Why can't I remember?

I know, there is something I want to say,
I feel it when I hear the little voice inside me whispering.
I know, my dreams are trying to tell me what's wrong,
I feel it when I wake up scared.
I know, somewhere in my mind, I'll find the answers I seek,
I feel it in my heart.
I know, there is a reason why I'm afraid of the truth,
I feel it in my thoughts and shattered dreams.
I know, there is a reason why I don't feel safe,
I feel it with every move I make.
I know, there is a reason why I feel uneasy with my body,
I feel it when I don't want to look in the mirror.

I know I am trying to run from something,
I am just not sure from what or why.
Why can't I remember?

I know, I must listen to my inner voice,
I know, I must remember my dreams,
I know, I must face my fears,
I know, I must open my mind, heart, and soul,
I know, I must stop running and look within,
Then, I will begin to remember.

—Heather Mesaric

$\mathcal{R}$emembering

Memories can surface whether we want them to or not. Some are so well hidden that we forget they ever existed in the first place. Take time to reflect on those memories that creep into the moment, they may be trying to tell you something.

~Heather Mesaric

The next step for me was remembering the past. This stage was very important to my recovery and also the most painful. I really had to push myself to go on and wanted to give up many times. I sincerely did not want to go back into all that pain. It seemed easier to pretend it never happened. In order to heal my wounds, I knew I had to look at the gruesome facts and unlock the secrets I was trying to hide from others and even myself. I believe abuse survivors use "forgetting" to avoid dealing with the pain we feel. I knew I had to get in touch with the memories and *make* myself remember.

At this point, I used my journal almost all the time. I began writing short sentences, poems, and meaningless words such as, kitchen, bathroom, outside, etc. I wrote everything down whether it made sense or not. On the streetcar travelling to and from work, in the bathroom or settling into bed at night, I wrote. My journal was with me constantly and I just kept writing.

After what seemed like forever, I began piecing together pictures from what I wrote. I looked at some of my thought patterns and was able to see that they had their roots in the events of my past, now pushing to the surface. Some seemed so far-fetched it was hard to imagine they had happened. I kept telling myself, "It's okay, these are only memories and they can't hurt you." They were horribly vivid and had been with me every day of my life. I didn't think I could ever forget them. The ones with the perpetual sexual advances were the worst, making me feel so helpless and shameful. I called them "the big picture." There were smaller events inside the big picture and I looked for links to try and understand what happened and why.

At a very early age I'd learned how to hide my true feelings so I knew I'd have to work hard to get in touch with my emotions surrounding the abuse. I'd become a great actress and no one could see that while I smiled at the world I was really crying with despair on the inside. I could be scared to death and no one would think anything was bothering me. *I hid my real feelings in order to survive.*

I had to reach into this pain and I would not allow myself to give up. Even though it was difficult for me, I kept working on healing the hurts. It was painful and scary but I kept going because I believed that once I got through the dark tunnel, I would see light. As I persevered, it was great to release all the baggage I'd been carrying and especially to let go of the guilt. It came together for me when I finally believed deep down that the abuse was not my fault—I did not ask for it, nor did I deserve to have it done to me. I urge you to have your support team close by as you work through the exercises in this stage. The comfort and help can make all the difference in the world.

Remembering the past stirred up many feelings that were locked away. I unleashed a floodgate of emotions that were hidden deep within me. I had so many feelings brewing inside me all at once, I was scared I wouldn't know how to get them all out. In addition, I kept saying to myself, "Why me? Really, Why me?"

Like most survivors I also found myself questioning the authenticity of the details I was remembering. Did the abuse really happen this way or was it my imagination? Was I remembering the true facts or was I making up false interpretations? I found myself questioning my recollections. I believed in my heart that I was remembering things quite accurately but self-sabotaging thoughts seemed to play games with my head.

I would not allow this doubt to get in the way of my healing. I was not going to languish in self-denial ever again. Most of my life I'd been down that path and I wanted the truth for myself and the rest of the world. I know what happened; my body knows what happened and so does my heart. It happened the way I remember it and that was that. *If you start doubting your memories,* allow yourself to believe in what you are thinking. There is definitely a reason you remember it this way. *Do not question yourself anymore. Believe in yourself, for once in your life.* Be your own best friend, love the person you are becoming and trust what you remember to be accurate.

You are healing, in your own special way, just as I was. Getting in touch with the bottled up feelings and emotions is your road away from the past and into your present and future life. This is *your* life; you own it; it is yours to rebuild. I certainly benefited from tearing down the walls between the agony of my past and where I stand in my life today. Remember, you are restructuring the present moment and creating a strong new foundation for your future.

Doing this work, I believed I was retrieving what was rightfully mine; my past, my truth and my lost childhood. I was going after the little girl who had been locked deep within me. It had been so many years since I'd closed that door and I loved meeting her again in this newfound setting. I brought her into the light and gave her love and hope.

As a victim of abuse, you have used many techniques to forget things in order to endure the pain. Now, use your memory to break the chains of denial and get in touch with the hurt. This is where real progress can start.

You have the strength to keep going. *You are a survivor*—you can do anything you want to. I believe if you kept your head above water during the abuse, you can find a way to heal your life. Just believe.

The process of remembering can be difficult and painful. You may need to do this unit several times in order to heal. However, it does get easier and the pain does subside as the wounds dissolve.

Remind yourself that you are not a victim any longer and what happened to you is now in the past. It can no longer hurt you, it's just memories. Put your past and those memories to rest—forever. Let go of the hurt and pain. Let yourself heal.

Keep saying to yourself: I am not alone; there are others who are healing from the same things that I am. Everyone who has completed this part of the book has just gone through similar experiences in order to heal from their past. I know you may be feeling a lot of anger at this time. This is very normal and believe it or not, you are recovering.

Journal Assignment: Write down all the feelings you want to express; feelings you have now and the ones you have hidden away in that dark place in your mind. Yes, those feelings you have had a really hard time asserting. Include any feelings of guilt, hate, fear, shame, sorrow, resentment, anger and anything else that surfaces.

To give yourself time to experience these emotions, do this assignment slowly. You may need to cry or shout to allow yourself to really feel. This is very important to the process so please give this work your full attention and effort. Write down everything about these feelings as they come up.

Journal Assignment—Exercise Two: Write down in short sentences what you remember about your abuse. This is a <u>critical stage</u> and requires your focus. Write down everything you remember; how often, with whom, what were your feelings at the time, before and afterwards. This exercise should be done gradually to give yourself time to remember. Be gentle with yourself and do not question what you write, just get your thoughts and memories on paper.

Journal Assignment—Exercise Three: Write the following sentences in your journal…

THE ABUSE WAS NOT MY FAULT.

I DID NOT ASK FOR THE ABUSE TO HAPPEN.

I DID NOT DESERVE THE ABUSE.

I DID NOT DO ANYTHING TO DESERVE THE ABUSE.

THE ABUSE WAS NOT MY FAULT

THE ABUSE WAS NOT MY FAULT.

Your Week's Affirmations: These are the ones that I used and found very helpful. For the next week say the following affirmations as often as possible, in order to create new patterns of "positive thinking." Some days I repeated them more than ten times in an hour or whenever I thought about them. My index cards really helped me to keep saying them often. Remember, you can create your own if these do not say what is in your heart.

Day one: I have the strength to reveal how I feel about the abuse.
Day two: I am remembering the pain and sorrow, but I am still safe.
Day three: I am now healing my life. I love who I am at this time.
Day four: I am a survivor; I have created a safe place for myself.
Day five: I am a survivor; I can do anything I choose to do.
Day six: I am allowing myself to have feelings. I remain safe.
Day seven: It is okay to release my feelings. I can handle these feelings.

Remember: you are healing; you are getting in touch with your feelings, and emotions, the ones you lost so long ago in order to deal with your pain. Yes, you can feel angry and resentful. You might even have pity. Whatever you are feeling at this time is what you should be feeling. It is your recovery process and it is happening this way because this is your road to a great future.

You are healing in your own special way and you can be proud of the hard work you have completed. It may not be easy but you are doing it. If you keep a journal of all those strange memories, thoughts and fears, you will find the key to solving the puzzle that is in your heart. Be patient and most of all soothe and comfort yourself when you have any unsettled thoughts.

The next healing unit will deal with the rage you may be experiencing at this time or may one day find yourself facing.

Fear

It comes and goes year after year,
I feel it coming, oh it is so very near.
It does not matter if I try to calm myself and say, oh dear,
I can hide my head and pretend I do not hear.
I can even try to hold back a tear,
However, I still have to deal with all this fear.

—Heather Mesaric

$\mathcal{F}$lashbacks

The things that happened to me in the past keep coming back to intimidate my reality. I cannot change the past… as these events helped to create the person I am today. However, I can change my perception of myself and not let the past influence my choices for today or for my future.

~Heather Mesaric

I wanted to put the abuse behind me and go on with my life. Looking for a magical answer and instant solutions, I didn't want to accept that flashbacks to painful memories would continue to surface. While I struggled with not wanting to deal with the abuse at all, I had pretended that it never occurred in the first place. I had wanted to forget it ever happened and now I had to keep saying to myself, "Yes, it did." I needed to feel the frustration, anger, fear, and embarrassment. Once I came to terms with the fact that I had been sexually and physically abused, my healing started to have meaning for me. I saw my world in a different way. This new found understanding gave my life a purpose.

I realized and understood that I am who I am today **because of the abuse**. It is part of my history and my distorted perception of family life. It is part of me and will always be a part of me; it's in the biography of my life.

Knowing that my life story included abuse, I had to acknowledge the flashbacks when they surfaced so that I didn't destroy my life and the future of my family. I needed to deal with these memories if I was ever going to change how I related to the people around me. It was how I saw myself becoming a better person, wife, mother, friend and family member. These memories helped validate my life. They contributed to the adult traits I have today and helped create who I am now.

At times, I didn't want to remember certain events. There was always abuse during festive times such as birthdays, Christmas, summer holidays, Easter and other special occasions. Children usually look forward to these festivities with joy and excitement. For me, it meant fear. I was always sexually or physically abused during these celebrations. In the early stages of my healing, I needed my support system more than ever when the holidays were approaching.

My friends and first husband were reassuring by changing how we spent the holidays and making them unique for our family. Today, I rejoice with such happiness and excitement that my children sometimes say "You're acting like a little kid, Mom; it's only Easter (or Christmas)." They don't realize that I am allowing myself the freedom to recapture a part of my childhood I never truly experienced. I continually re-live and change my view of these special events to help mould my children's histories as we all cherish the good times. I give my children the wonderful traditions and anticipation that I was cheated out of so long ago.

As the memories surfaced, I had to remind myself that I was not imagining what was coming up. It took courage to stop myself from minimizing the experiences. Many times I found myself saying, "It couldn't have happened that way." or "It wasn't that bad."

Other times, I would question whether it really ever happened. I didn't want to believe that it did, yet I knew I hadn't invented the memories that kept haunting me. They were true. They were a record of my past that needed to be dealt with and put to rest. The only way I knew how to do this was to remember them and put meaning to them. I wasn't sure how I was going to go about it, but just that it had to be done.

As I continued to allow the memories to come to light I learned things about myself, some good, some not so good. I learned the flashbacks could not hurt me unless I let them. Through determination, I found ways to deal with the pain and confusion. I realized that the healing process would bring up memories that I may not want to face but taking control of my thoughts, trusting and believing in myself, I knew I could handle anything I had to. I allowed myself to get upset or angry if I felt like it and to seek advice and comfort from my support system. I took control of my life so that the past could not hurt me any more. I learned to take each situation, memory or fear and evaluate it to uncover new ways of understanding its meaning. I began to realize that I am a very special person in my own way *because* of the abuse. It is part of my life's blueprint and will always remain with me. I must accept this in order to change and acknowledge who I am.

Healing from my abuse is a lifelong process. The effects continue to unravel themselves and they never occur in the same manner as the last time. As I healed, I began to notice that I remembered more and became aware of many unresolved feelings. I knew my healing process would have to be unique to my needs. We all deal with situations differently. Therefore, everyone heals in their own way. Your process could be entirely different from mine even though you might feel similar feelings. It all depends on how you handle changes in your life and the quality of your support system. Your memory of the abuse may become clearer and incidents may be triggered at any time. They could happen when someone touches your arm in an innocent way, while watching a television program, smelling certain foods, flowers, perfume, or even when someone speaks in a particular tone of voice.

These flashbacks are quite normal and it is healthy to bring them into the open. Trauma can be blocked from our consciousness to enable us to go on. You may have become numb, pushing your feelings and pain into hiding so that no one could ever hurt you again. Now you need to bring them out into the open for resolution. As you heal, you will not be able to resist the memories of what truly happened. You are not going crazy and they are not made up stories. You are regaining the inner child you locked away so long ago. Allow yourself to go through this process no matter how overwhelming it may feel. Talk to your support group about your feelings. Unlock the doors that keep you from living your life as you were meant to live it.

The more you expose the hidden hurts, the sooner you will sort out the confusion and make the healing process easier. Let yourself feel all the emotions that surface during this stage. Yes, that's right; it's just a stage you are going through. Bringing anything into the light makes it more manageable. Eventually you will heal the pain, conquer your fears and recover your true identity. The most important advice I can give you is to remind you that the memories cannot hurt you. They may make you scared, angry, or depressed but ultimately, if you stand up to them, they cannot hurt you. You must realize that you can no longer suppress the memories if you want to heal yourself. Believe me, when you get it all out, you will feel much better about the world and especially about yourself.

Journal Assignment: Buy a small notebook that fits into your pocket or purse. On the top of the page, write these columns Date, Time, Memory, Trigger (what triggered the memory). Use this book to make quick reference notes as your memories come up. Here's an example:

Date	Time	Memory	Trigger
Apr. 5	6:00pm	Being beaten by my father for not wanting to eat something	My child not eating her vegetables
Dec. 19	9:00am	Being touched by my caregiver	Watching a man walking hand-in-hand with his granddaughter.

Keep writing in your little notebook. The point is to see how often your thoughts go back to the memories. Write your feelings about this exercise and your reactions in your journal. How did they make you feel? What did you want to do when you had the memory? What did you actually do? What could you change to make it easier the next time? In upcoming units you will learn some techniques to help release anger and stress.

Your Week's Affirmations: These are the ones that I used and found very helpful. For the next week say the following affirmations as often as possible, in order to create new patterns of "positive thinking." Some days I repeated them more than ten times in an hour or whenever I thought about them. My index cards really helped me to keep saying them often. Remember, you can create your own if these do not say what is in your heart.

Day one: I allow the memories to surface.
Day two: My memories are from the past, I learn who I am from them.
Day three: Memories help me understand who I am today.
Day four: I trust that my flashbacks are true and real.
Day five: I believe in my memories and myself.
Day six: I accept my memories as part of my history.
Day seven: My knowledge of the abuse makes me stronger.

Remember: Memories are recorded messages of what we have seen, spoken, heard, and witnessed. They are made up of events that have affected our lives in some way and can be anything from wonderful to tragic. Ask yourself, "Will this memory help or hinder my progress with my healing journey? Will it bring happiness, peace and even closure?" If you find a recollection continues to create extremely painful or other negative feelings, then re-do an exercise to release the emotion. If it still needs more attention refer to the tasks in the unit called "Clearing The Closet Of The Mind" (Page 117). I found that I had to repeat this process several times to decrease the intensity of some reactions. I am now to the point where some memories are nothing more than me looking out the window of my car, just passing thoughts. They are here and gone in such quick succession they hold little meaning for me.

*B*laming Ourselves

Absolve yourself from the blame that is not yours, it will allow you to be free.

~Heather Mesaric

Next on my agenda was to look at how and why I blamed myself for the abuse. I always believed that I must have somehow asked for it or that I could have prevented it from occurring. Somewhere deep down I did know that I hadn't deserved to be treated with such violence or disrespect. My abusers considered me an object of sexual play for themselves. Young children can easily misinterpret mixed messages from adults and I questioned my role all the time.

I knew that in order to heal, I needed to get rid of my feelings of blame and guilt. I needed to learn to stop. It was not my fault. It happened to me without my consent and I truly did not know how to stop it. I had no way of preventing the abuse and found through experimentation that I could not stop it when I tried. It was clear that I needed to really grasp the message that it was not my fault and stop punishing myself. I had to stop this self-blame once and for all.

Journal Assignment: Write some of the reasons why you think you are to blame for the abuse and the ways you keep punishing yourself for what happened. What kinds of things do you say to yourself about your role in the abuse? Write down the ways that you constantly put yourself

61

down. What names do you call yourself? What are the hurtful things you say about yourself? Write it all down on paper so you can see what it is you have been believing both consciously and unconsciously.

Journal Assignment—**Exercise Two:** Read over what you wrote in the previous assignment. Take a very honest look at what you have written. Go over it several times to thoroughly comprehend what you have been telling yourself.

Journal Assignment—**Exercise Three:** NOW write *"I was not to blame for the abuse. I was not to blame for the abuse."* Read it out loud repeatedly until you begin to sincerely believe that you were **not** responsible.

As you write, be sure you understand that you did the best that you could to protect yourself. I believe right or wrong, we do things for a number of reasons at any given moment. Yes, we make bad choices, and we can learn from them. We also learn from other people's mistakes and in the case of abuse, sometimes lessons they say we need to learn.

"You did not ask to be abused. It was not your fault."

Once I stopped blaming myself for the abuse, I found that I no longer blamed myself for everything else that was going wrong in my life. I stopped punishing myself and became more aware of how I was hurting and putting myself down in most everyday situations. I learned to be less critical and more forgiving of myself. I was also beginning to like myself and looked for the good rather than the bad in myself and others. Indeed, I was changing in a positive way and could see and feel the difference.

Your Week's Affirmations: These are the ones that I used and found very helpful. For the next week say the following affirmations as often as possible, in order to create new patterns of "positive thinking." Some days I repeated them more than ten times in an hour or whenever I thought about them. My index cards really helped me to keep saying them often. Remember, you can create your own if these do not say what is in your heart.

Day one: I believe the abuse was not my fault.

Day two: I believe that the abuse was not my fault.

Day three: I accept the fact that the abuse was not my fault.

Day four: I know the abuse was not my fault.

Day five: I embrace the knowledge that the abuse was not my fault.

Day six: I nurture and cherish the truth that the abuse was not my fault.

Day seven: I release the need to blame myself for the abuse.

Remember: It may take time for you to stop accusing and blaming yourself for allowing the abuse to take place. You must put this terrible misconception to rest. You were not responsible and you have the ability to let these feelings go. Be gentle with yourself and treat yourself with the dignity that you deserve. Over the past few chapters you have done a lot of deep, exploratory work. Now, you may be noticing some real changes taking place in your life. Celebrate your progress by sharing these changes with your support team. Buy yourself a symbol of success such as a long stemmed red rose, a small angel pin or something else to pamper yourself. Show yourself how much you love who you are and who you are becoming.

$\mathcal{E}$nraged/Anger

Anger is an emotion that has a mind of its own, such as a wild beast lashing out at everything that comes near it. We must learn to have self-discipline in order to bring it under our control.

~Heather Mesaric

Eventually I knew I had to deal with the feelings of outrage at what I had brought to the surface. I also knew that I wanted to get control over my anger at the persons who sexually abused me. I found the more I thought about what happened, the angrier I became. Most of the time I wished they were dead because the greatest betrayal was that they were family; the people I should have been able to trust. This feeling of hatred occurred day in and day out. I used to fantasize that they would die a very painful death and I became obsessed with my rage towards them.

My anger towards my abusers was also being projected onto every man I came in contact with. I would yell or say rude and awful things to them. I was beginning to enjoy hurting and manipulating them. My belief about how a relationship should work was so distorted because I could not let go of my hate. This was when I really knew I had to do something about how I thought and felt about men. I wanted to learn new ways to express my hurt and disappointment without directing it at innocent bystanders. This was not easy for me. It required a great deal of patience and determination to learn how to handle my anger.

The good news is that I succeeded, and you will too. Remember: you do not want or need to be out of control with your anger. These emotions do nothing but keep you immobilized and the unleashed feelings can be very unhealthy. Anger is such a powerful emotion that it can destroy a relationship and distort reality. It can take over your life to the point where you really do not have control over what happens to you.

Releasing your anger is the best way to control it. Up to now you have been working on getting in touch with your feelings and the next step is learning how to deal with the anger. If you don't, your anger will be aimed inappropriately at the wrong people (including yourself) for all the wrong reasons. You may say things that you do not mean or that are hurtful. You may even blame them for things that were not their fault. These are some of the harmful behaviours that manifest when anger is out of control.

You have every right to be angry, but you do not have the right to be angry at the world. Your loved ones do not deserve to be mistreated either. By all means, be angry at the culprit(s), in the right way and for the right amount of time. Don't let this hate take over your life forever. You deserve peace and closure.

Let me share with you the way I learned to release anger. It began with taking ownership of my life and my feelings. I allowed myself the opportunity to say what I wanted to say even though the abusers were no longer present. As well, I changed my attitude towards myself and the people around me. I admitted to myself, whom I was really angry at. It was not my friends, my immediate family or myself. I was angry at the specific men who had hurt me in the past and taken away my childhood. It was the men who made me feel dirty and worthless and treated me as though I had no human rights. I was *furious* with *them* for what they had done *to me*.

J**ournal Assignment:* Make a list of everything that makes you angry about the abuse. For example: "…when he touched my breasts" or "when he held me down and I could not get out of his grip." etc. Be as specific as you can and give the names of every abuser. Your angry feelings may come from not remembering exactly what happened, or from feeling guilty about what you do remember. Write down who you are angry at and for what reason. When the list is done, read it over. Did you include everything? Is there anything or anyone else you want to add to this list? Be sure you have been completely honest. ***Now, prepare to release your anger.

***J**ournal Assignment—Exercise Two:* Read aloud the list of names from the previous exercise, one at a time, as if you were talking to the person who committed the assault. In your mind see them face-to-face with you and say, "(Name), I hate (or, am angry at) you because you (briefly describe the abusive event). Because of what you did to me, my life has been (fill in the consequence of their actions). Take a deep breath (as many times as you need to) and say softly, "I release my anger towards you for what you did. I no longer need to be angry or outraged at you. I release this anger from my body." While you are saying these statements, picture in your mind the anger being washed down the drain of your sink or taken out to sea on a wave. Feel the anger leaving you. You must continue this until you release each and every person on the list. Go through this process repeatedly until you feel you have let go of all of your anger. It may take a long time, but the process will free you in the end. I personally felt very relieved (and exhausted) after completing this exercise.

***Y**our Week's Affirmations:* These are the ones that I used and found very helpful. For the next week say the following affirmations as often as possible, in order to create new patterns of "positive thinking." Some days I repeated them more than ten times in an hour or whenever I thought about them. My index cards really helped me to keep saying them often. Remember, you can create your own if these do not say what is in your heart.

Day one: I let go of my anger. I let go of my anger.
Day two: It is safe for me to release my anger.
Day three: I release my anger. I release my outrage.
Day four: I release the need to be angry all the time.
Day five: I let go of my anger and move forward with my life.
Day six: I release my anger in positive ways.

Day seven: I let go of my feelings of being out-of-control.

Remember: When you find new memories surfacing which bring up anger or resentment, use these affirmations and exercises to release the sensations. Be your own guiding force. You will know what you need. If you are still feeling some small hints of anger, be gentle with yourself. Upcoming units such as "Releasing The Anger" will be very helpful in dissipating these stubborn areas. You deserve the best and you can give yourself the love you need. Tell yourself that you are special and you are lovable. Give yourself a hug and kiss your hand as you would a child's, with tenderness and meaning. Embrace who you are today, enjoy who you are becoming.

$\mathcal{R}$eleasing The Anger

When anger continues to fester in your life, you have to find a productive way to let it escape in order for a new and creative life to emerge.

~*Heather Mesaric*

Although I worked very hard, I was unable to release all my rage towards the men in my past. After completing the last unit of exercises, I still found I needed something more. It felt important that they know how I was feeling and how much they had hurt me. I decided to write a letter that would express my feelings and unburden all of my hurts, disappointment, and resentment.

The main purpose of the letter was to get my rage onto paper. I wrote pages upon pages of how I felt. I let it all out and didn't worry about spelling, grammar or whether or not I made sense. I just kept writing, crying, writing, crying and writing and crying some more. I wrote until I could not write anymore and until I'd said everything I ever wanted to say.

Personally, I noticed that after I wrote this letter I was not nearly as angry as I had been. While writing the letter it was helpful to punch my pillow with my fists to avenge my honour and scream, "Take this, you S.O.B.!" Then I would write, "You bastard this is what you did!" I'd hit the pillow again, and write some more. A tremendous amount of hate and revengeful feelings came out during my letter writing and pillow-pounding.

When the letter was finally finished, I read it several times over the next few days. I added things I had forgotten to mention that I felt were necessary to let them know what I was really thinking. Each time I read the letter or made changes to it, I felt better. One of the last times I read it, I actually started feeling pity for my abusers. I found myself thinking what losers they were. I was still angry at what they did to me, but I no longer had the strong intensity of rage. My reaction was much less explosive and it was by now, a relief to know that my anger was not out-of-control.

My final reading of the letter was done looking in the mirror. Pretending I was reading it to my abusers, I let them have it all. My anger poured out and I held nothing back. I told them how I felt, what I hoped would happen to them, and I said my good-bye. I went back to my journal and wrote, "I am free. My life is my own from this moment on. I am free."

Journal Assignment: Write a letter to the person(s) who abused you and do not hold back any feelings. Remember, spelling, grammar and sentence structure do not matter, just get out all the emotions. Say *anything* you want and if it helps, use bad language and be as nasty with name-calling or remarks, as you need to be. Write about all the hurts, disappointments, anger and the retaliatory things you would like to happen to them. Fill as many pages as you want. Don't limit yourself or feel you have "done enough". Pay attention to whatever is still simmering inside. Write with as much passion as you need to release the emotion and ultimately feel better. *Get those feelings out.* After you have written the letter(s) move on to the next exercises as soon as possible. If you can set aside a whole day or even a weekend alone it will be very helpful in completing this work. If you need some time in between to fulfill family or work obligations put the letter(s) in a safe place as you will need it for exercises in upcoming units.

Journal Assignment—Exercise Two: Now write a short letter asking for an apology and an explanation from the person(s) who abused you. State in your letter what you want to hear from them. Be as specific as you can. Write down what you think you need to hear in order to let go of the guilt, shame or hurt. **Please note:** this exercise can bring up many underlying feelings. It may spark more anger, sadness or hopelessness. These feelings are very normal and are part of the healing process. Relax after this exercise and be sure to praise yourself for all you have accomplished. Nurture yourself by doing something special that makes you feel clean and whole. Take a hot bath or shower or maybe a dip into a cold pool or lake. Whatever you choose, wash off the negative energy that was once a part of you. At this time it is essential that you repeat over and over, "I love myself" until you feel it in your soul.

Your Week's Affirmations: These are the ones that I used and found very helpful. For the next week say the following affirmations as often as possible, in order to create new patterns of "positive thinking," Some days I repeated them more than ten times in an hour or whenever I thought about them. My index cards really helped me to keep saying them often. Remember, you can create your own if these do not say what is in your heart.

Day one: I release my anger in a positive way.
Day two: I love myself now and forever.
Day three: I respect and understand my feelings of anger.
Day four: I acknowledge and release my anger in a positive way.
Day five: I express my anger in a healthy manner.
Day six: I express my anger so it will not hurt others or myself.
Day seven: I release my past. I welcome my new life as a loving person.

Remember: There are many ways in which to release your anger. You can pound or scream into a pillow, sit in your car (in private) and shout with the music turned up loud, swing a baseball bat in the air or kick your legs at a punching bag. Play dough is a great stress reliever and a small chunk of clay can be twisted and torn apart. Just be careful not to ever allow your anger release to affect other people. I encourage you to think of more ways that may be useful in helping you release your anger.

*F*orgiving Yourself And Others

Saying "I forgive you," are the three hardest words to say and mean.
However, when spoken they have the power to change anything.

~Heather Mesaric

Deep down inside, I felt something needed to be resolved. I had this nagging feeling that I wanted more closure for what had happened to me. I struggled with the sense that there had been no explanation or apology from the abusers. Even though it would not change what had happened and might not make things "right," I felt that I needed some acknowledgement from them. Validation of my memories was very important to me to prove to myself and others that I had not made up the events and that I was not responsible. Realistically I knew I would never get this because they would not confess and some of my abusers had even passed away.

To go on with my healing I had to find a way to fulfill my request with or without their help. I would have to give myself what I wanted most from them.

I re-read the letter from the last unit (Releasing The Anger) Journal Assignment—Exercise Two where I asked for an apology from my abuser. Then I wrote a reply from my abuser that said everything I wanted to hear. This was terribly demanding for me because I had to put myself in their position and imagine that they were remorseful. I envisioned what they would say and the excuses they would make for their actions. *I needed this letter for my own satisfaction so while I knew they would never have written it; I intentionally focused on what I wanted to hear.*

The following letter is a sample of what I wrote to myself from one of my abusers:

Dear Heather:

I received your letter, and want you to know how deeply sorry I am that you have lived all these years with the pain I caused you. I had no right to ruin your life. It was very selfish of me to take away your innocence and to expose you to the horrible things I did.

I truly am ashamed of my behaviour and wrongdoing. I did not mean to hurt you the way I did. It is very hard for me to put into words what I was thinking at the time of the abuse. I know this isn't easy for you to understand, but I was not thinking about how I was hurting you. I was only thinking of myself and what I was getting out it.

I am sorry for so many things. I'm sorry for not being there for you, for taking away your adolescence, for making you wear things you really did not like. I am sorry for making your life a living hell. If I could take it back, I would. I want you to know I am really sorry.

Sincerely John Doe

Journal Assignment: Now it's your turn. Re-read the letter you wrote to your abuser(s). Reply to yourself from one or more of them. Answer these questions the way you think they would, including the excuses and denial that may come forward. What do you think they would say if they wrote to you with an explanation? Would they give you an apology? (If not, don't worry, you can still heal without it. I knew I would never get justification from my abusers and did not let that stop me.) *Write the letter you want to receive from them.* Give yourself the apology and anything more you have been waiting to hear.

Now, mail the letter to yourself. Yes, mail the letter to yourself. Remember you are putting the wheels in motion so you can achieve your goal of healing. This is a very symbolic gesture and will help you believe your way through this journey. (When it arrives, do not open the letter – wait for instructions in exercise three.)

After reviewing the letter asking my abuser for an apology I was surprised to find that, I also wanted an apology from myself. I needed to let go of the guilt I was feeling and pour love into my empty heart. For years I'd blamed myself for not doing things "right," by not defending myself and for not finding help when I needed it most. I knew I would have to forgive myself and acknowledge that I wasn't responsible for what happened. It was a big step to release the shame and allow myself to be forgiven. In spite of all I knew there was a lingering belief that somehow, in some way, I had deserved what I got.

Journal Assignment—Exercise Two: *Now comes a step that I really resisted and found quite hard to complete.* Stand in front of a mirror and say out loud "I forgive you *(Stating your own name)*," Say this over and over again. Wrap your arms around your shoulders, hold and love yourself. Continue to say, "I forgive you …" until you feel inside the possibilities for self-forgiveness. (I never cried so much or as deeply during my work as I did doing this exercise.)

You may need to do this over the course of a few days or on several different occasions to begin to feel the power of forgiving yourself. This task can be formidable because it demands that we do something for ourselves that we may not believe is possible. Just continue telling your-self, "I forgive you …."

The next two exercises (3 & 4) can be done with one of your support team members if you think they can help you through them.

Journal Assignment—Exercise Three: When you have completed the previous exercise to your full satisfaction you can move on to this one. In front of a mirror, open the "apology" letter you wrote from your abuser and look at yourself as you read the letter out loud. Envision the abusers face and him saying the words to you. Get in touch with the feelings that are emerging. Re-read the letter as many times as necessary to feel you are really immersed in the experience. Now, write in your journal all the feelings that came up and notice if anger and hurt have re-surfaced. Continue to write down how you are feeling and be very thorough.

Journal Assignment—Exercise **Four:** Do not move on **until you have completed the above exercise.** Facing the mirror, read the abuser's response letter out loud once more. Then, looking into your eyes, imagine you are talking to your abuser. As you talk, pretend you are blowing up a balloon. (Use a real balloon if you want more effect, but it's not necessary to complete the exercise.) With each breath you blow into the balloon say out loud "I forgive you (person's name);" blow into the balloon again and repeat, "I forgive you (name)." Do this until the balloon is fully inflated. Pretend to, or actually tie the balloon. Go outside, take a deep breath and let go of the balloon. As you release it (whether it's real or imaginary), say one last time "I forgive you (name)." Watch the balloon floating away, and visualize all your hate, anger and vengeful feelings going with it. Repeat the exercise for each of your abusers. Do it as often as you need to in order to release whatever is preventing you from forgiving your abuser(s).

Your Weeks Affirmations: These are the ones that I used and found very helpful. For the next week say the following affirmations as often as possible, in order to create new patterns of "positive thinking." Some days I repeated them more than ten times in an hour or whenever I thought about them. My index cards really helped me to keep saying them often. Remember, you can create your own if these do not say what is in your heart.

Day one: I forgive myself. I am not to blame.
Day two: It is okay to forgive both others and myself.
Day three: I forgive others for their wrongdoing.
Day four: I am a loving and caring person. I can forgive.
Day five: I only have loving thoughts about myself.
Day six: I allow myself the ability to forgive and love again.
Day seven: I have the strength to forgive. I am able to let go.

Remember: Forgiveness does not come easy for most people, even those who have not been abused. Be kind to yourself if this takes several attempts before you feel genuine forgiveness has taken place. While you are doing the exercises give yourself permission to cry or scream out if you need to. Hug yourself throughout these exercises and if moments of doubt creep back in, just say, "I forgive you" and let it go.

Trust

Trust is a word that means "have faith" …have faith in yourself and others. It means, putting aside your fears and doubts in order to repair the damage that the abuse has caused. Only then, can the path to a better life be found.

~Heather Mesaric

At this point, I began to deal with my lack of trust. Having been betrayed so many times over the years I did not trust others at all. Another serious obstacle for me was that I did not trust myself. I'd been told I was wrong so often that I was never quite sure if I could believe what went on in my head and even my heart.

I had to learn how to trust and to be trustworthy. It seemed very risky in light of my past. I knew that once I trusted myself I could move forward in learning to trust others.

Trust is earned and once given, should be handled with great respect. You have already begun trusting both yourself and others with the work you have completed. You have trusted yourself to remember the past and to fulfill your obligations in your Life Contract. You have trusted others by including them in your support system and perhaps participating in some of the exercise work with you. For a moment, put aside your fears and consider the possibility of trusting yourself and others. While it is healthy and normal to be somewhat "on guard" you need to move past the restrictive behaviour that can manifest as paranoia when we don't trust at all. This is a big step and you can encourage yourself by saying, "I've come this far; why should I stop now?"

The first person you need to establish a trusting relationship with is yourself. In order to trust, you must prove to yourself that you are indeed trustworthy. You have laid an excellent foundation through the exercises in the previous units. Be proud of your progress and give yourself credit for implementing this new way of thinking.

Journal Assignment: Write down all the times when you did what you said you were going to do for yourself. For example, think of times when you said you would do something self-nurturing and you did it. Include times when you believed what you were feeling. Describe any occasions when you followed through on changing an attitude or behaviour that was self-defeating. Show how you can trust yourself to be supportive when self-doubt creeps in and listen to a supportive inner voice.

Journal Assignment—**Exercise Two:** Write down all the times when you did what you said you were going to do for someone else. This may be calling your friends when you said you would, helping a neighbour when you agreed to, paying your bills on time, going to work regularly, completing tasks you said you'd do, etc. You may surprise yourself with an endless list of times that you could be relied on to fulfill your obligations. Think of things people count on you for and especially ones where you know they come to you because you won't let them down. When your list is done (and don't rush it – give yourself lots of room to expand) look it over to reinforce to yourself that you are definitely trustworthy. You may even want to state emphatically, "Yes, I can be trusted." Your natural instincts are your greatest asset. There may be times when your inner voice is cautionary and it's important that you listen. Allow your body to communicate your feelings about what is happening around you and trust yourself when the message you hear is, "Hey this is great!"

Journal Assignment—**Exercise Three:** Now it's time to write down the situations when other people did what they said they would do. Consider friends, neighbours, co-workers and relatives including your children. When you have a long and complete list, compare it with the previous one. Notice that there have been and still are many times when you can trust others.

Your Week's Affirmations: These are the ones that I used and found very helpful. For the next week say the following affirmations as often as possible, in order to create new patterns of "positive thinking." Some days I repeated them more than ten times in an hour or whenever I thought about them. My index cards really helped me to keep saying them often. Remember, you can create your own if these do not say what is in your heart.

Day one: I trust myself to make good choices.
Day two: I believe in myself. I am trustworthy.
Day three: I am truthful to others and myself.
Day four: I trust myself and those around me.
Day five: I am very trustworthy.
Day six: I am dependable, reliable and trustworthy.
Day seven: I believe that everything I do and say is trustworthy.

Remember: You have control over your life and make good choices for yourself. Trusting yourself and others gives you the power to overcome any situation that comes up. You have the strength to prove that you are the best that you can be. I believe that we do our best that we can in every situation that is presented to us at any given time.

As you continue to heal, the roller-coaster ride won't seem as scary and out-of-control. During painful times be sure to hug yourself and heap on lots of praise and support. Be loving and remember that you do deserve to be loved. Love is the ultimate gift you can give to yourself, so, go ahead and cherish the new you. Say to yourself often, "I love you!" Praise yourself and know that others have taken this journey before you. You are not alone and with time and effort, you will heal the wounds and be free.

*T*aking Risks

Change can bring new opportunities that offer creative and inspiring ideas or beliefs. It can help to overcome the fear of the unknown, which hinders individuals from going forward in their lives.

~Heather Mesaric

Being a survivor has pushed me to take risks that I might otherwise not have. Writing this book was the biggest non-secure venture I've ever taken. *You* have also taken a risk by buying, reading and completing the exercises in this book. You decided to believe in yourself and enter into the healing process. Each phase you go through allows you to learn more about yourself, your strengths, weaknesses, fears, doubts and your willingness to overcome any obstacle you encounter. To some, a risk might be moving to a new city or switching careers. To others it can be more personal such as risking rejection from those we love by standing up for ourselves. We cannot avoid taking risks in our everyday lives and must decide which ones are worth the consequences that every action produces.

If you were young when you were abused, it was the abuser who determined the risk. To some extent, a victim sometimes has to make a choice and weigh the pros and cons of being "available". For example, I learned that taking a risk and telling my teacher at school resulted in catastrophic consequences. After that, I knew it was just too risky to speak up.

The reactions can be split into two different types of behaviour. One, is those who become very guarded, withdrawn, and angry. The other is when victims become bold risk takers with an attitude of nothing to lose. I fell into the latter category and rarely thought through the potential repercussions of my deeds. Most often, I ended up regretting the decisions I had made with reckless abandon.

Now, I am definitely more realistic when making a choice. A long process needed to unfold before I was able to make good choices for myself. I explored why I was so willing to jump into situations without a single concern for what might happen to me. Asking myself, "Why am I doing this?" was very frightening for me. I took a hard look at my habits and destructive patterns. Areas in which I knew I had made poor choices were with my job, my first marriage and what I wanted to accomplish with my life. They seemed to be the right decisions when I made them, but with a new sense of self they no longer served my best interests. Facing the risk of reversing some of these decisions and making more appropriate changes was definitely daunting.

I believe that most of the time when we are making a decision we honestly feel it is the right one for us. Otherwise, we might choose differently. There are also times when we know intuitively that it's not the best for us, however, we still proceed because the risk of not doing so is much greater. In hindsight, it may seem that we made the wrong decision, but given the same circumstances we would likely do it again because we believed it was the *right decision to make at that time.*

When I looked at some of the choices I had made, one of the results was that it became clear I needed to end my marriage. The relationship had deteriorated and was unhealthy for us both. We moved every year, sold our homes after each separation and lived a very unstable life, to say the least. In spite of a lot of hard work, especially by my ex-husband, we just could not make it viable and eventually divorced.

Then I changed jobs, fell in love with my second husband (whom I believe is my soul mate) and moved into a home where I have remained for over 14 years. It took a lot of soul-searching and risk-taking to transform my life in such a profound way.

Being willing to take big chances changed my life forever and was integral to my healing. You may have to explore your own life situations and possibly make some major adjustments in your lifestyle or circumstances. It's important to examine every area of your life to see what nurtures and what depletes you. Whether it's going back to school or getting specific counselling, don't be afraid of risks that in due time will empower you.

Journal Assignment: Ask yourself some questions to invoke a deeper understanding of who you are and what you really want out of your life. Be very honest with your answers even if they cause some painful feelings. You are working towards developing a confident, strong character and becoming mentally, spiritually and emotionally mature.

Do these exercises slowly; it may take you several journal entries to answer all the questions.

If you decide to change your answers after reading what you wrote, that's fine. The more honest you are with yourself the more you will learn. Securing a healthy understanding of your wants and needs leads you to seeing what is preventing you from making changes in your life. The first question is "What are your reasons for doing what you do?" In other words, what is motivating your behaviours? We have different reasons for doing what we do and you need to consider whether or not your rationale is helpful or harmful. Look at everyday situations and activities to trace the thread of connection between intention and action. (If you check back to your answers several months from now you may be surprised to discover they are no longer relevant.)

You may want to ask yourself, "Why do I continue doing something that is hurtful to me?" A series of questions that naturally come up are "What purpose does this serve?" "What am I getting out of what I am doing?" and most of all, "Do I want to change this behaviour?" If you answer yes, put together a list of options so that you have a strong, vivid understanding of why you want to make the changes.

Another important question to ask yourself is "Can I do this alone or do I need help?" Sometimes we need others for support or guidance. Call those you have trusted with your story to help you be clear with your responses. This exercise can be done many times during the healing process and used to move through any set of events.

Journal Assignment—**Exercise Two:** Answer the following questions in your journal. Give lots of details and include all the possible answers that come to mind.

1) Are you happy with your life (why or why not)?

2) What changes would you make if you could? How would your life be different if you could change it? Write it down, as you want it to be. Go ahead, be a dreamer; the world is at your feet.

3) What changes do you want to make in your career, your home, your partner, and your friendships? What do you want out of this life?

4) What outside help do you need to make these changes: i.e. friends, family, therapist etc? Who can really help you achieve your goals?

5) What limitations or situations have **stopped** you from making these changes in the past? What are the obstacles you have to overcome to achieve them now? Is it money, time, confidence, worry, fear, education? What else is holding you back or preventing you from changing your life? Is one of the answers – yourself? Be honest.

6) How much time do you require to make the changes—i.e. a day, week, month, year? Be as realistic as possible.

7) Do you know where to go for local resources to help you make changes—i.e. where to go for money for education purposes? Is there a free program offered at your library? Do you know how to find a good therapist that you can work with?

8) Do you put yourself down with negative statements and thoughts? What are they? Make a list of all the awful things you say to yourself or think about yourself. You may have made a few even while doing this exercise. If so, what are they, and what do you believe about yourself?

9) Do you allow others the opportunity to help you? If not, why not? Are you willing to ask for help to make some of these changes? If so, why? If not, then why not?

10) What do you like about yourself? What would you like to change? Is this possible? If not, why not? If you cannot make the changes you feel are necessary, ask yourself why you have not accepted this perceived inadequacy. Remember, there are two sides to every coin. You can always turn a negative thought into a positive one. It is all

in the way you think or feel about yourself. What could you do to make this so-called defect more acceptable and tolerable for you? For example, I always wanted to be taller than my 5'2". I discovered I could do several things to make myself look and feel taller. Simple modifications to my appearance made me feel more beautiful and less concerned about my actual height.

***Y**our Week's Affirmations:* These are the ones that I used and found very helpful. For the next week say the following affirmations as often as possible, in order to create new patterns of "positive thinking." Some days I repeated them more than ten times in an hour or whenever I thought about them. My index cards really helped me to keep saying them often. Remember, you can create your own if these do not say what is in your heart.

Day one: I am learning more about myself everyday.
Day two: I know that making changes will enhance my life.
Day three: I allow myself the opportunity to change.
Day four: I always make good choices for myself.
Day five: Making changes allows me to discover new things.
Day six: Making changes with my life is important for me.
Day seven: I love the changes I am making with my life.

R**emember:* Some changes are more difficult than others and take a little longer to achieve. Allow the situation to take its natural course while you explore and discover the best possible changes for you. This is not the time to be impatient. Just as a seed needs time to grow into a beautiful flower, it takes time for changes to occur within you. Be gentle with yourself during the waiting period. ***Think of yourself as a butterfly in its cocoon. Be patient and learn to enjoy your newfound journey of life. Love yourself for who you are at this given moment. Embrace the changes that are occurring and those yet to come.

My advice to you is to dream big. Go after something that you truly want to happen. Make as many changes as you feel you need to in order to give yourself the life you desire and deserve. If you believe strongly enough about something it will come about. Believe me, I've lived it.

You are holding my biggest dream (this book). However, I was also my major critic. My self-talk said, "Yeah right! You write a book? Dream on. You couldn't write a book if your life depended on it." I struggled to overcome the negative thinking, stayed the course and my book is living proof that dreams do come true. Reminding myself often that I was writing this book to help others helped me face my fears and self-doubts. I am so proud of my accomplishments and for taking the risks to see my vision through. Go ahead, **_dream big_** and never give up. Believe in yourself and take a chance on you. This is your life to enjoy, transform, and make a reality.

*H*ealing Takes Time

If we stop long enough to enjoy the person we are, we just might find something about ourselves that we like.

~*Heather Mesaric*

I believe the work completed in the previous units is the foundation of your healing journey. You needed to explore, recover and get control of the areas that have created havoc for you before further healing can take place.

Something that needs to be emphasized is the importance of allowing the process of healing to move at a pace that feels comfortable for you. We are all unique and have our own circumstances that dictate how quickly we work through various issues. Be gentle with yourself and don't expect more than what is reasonable for you. Let yourself work slowly a second time through any of the units you feel you can benefit from repeating. Once you are satisfied that you have completed each unit, then, and only then, move on with the knowledge that you have done your best to heal the wounds of the past.

Throughout my healing process, I found myself going over the last 7 units several times and re-doing many of the exercises. With each review, I discovered I went deeper into lost memories and gained more emotional strength to handle the past and present. To this day, I use the exercises and affirmations to cope with triggered feelings or to explore a re-awakened, stubborn memory.

There may be times when you want to re-do one of the units, especially when you are faced with flashbacks. When this happens, it's important not to retreat into old patterns of suppressing the feelings. Read the unit that best applies to how you are feeling at the time to re-affirm your understanding of yourself. Remember, this book is meant to be a life-long companion, helping you heal and giving you positive alternatives to negative thinking and despair.

Another tip during difficult times is to post notes around your home, car, and office to remind yourself of the positive changes you have achieved. These might include statements such as "I have the strength to change my life and how I feel about myself," "I love myself," "I am great" and "Keep up the good work." You might even say, "Congratulations. You've come a long way!" **Write anything that is positive.** These notes were taped all over my house and everywhere I'd be able to see them often. We are bombarded with messages in our every day lives so it makes sense to put positive affirmations right up front. You have the power to overcome any situation or thought you have. Just believe in yourself and remember you are on the right track.

What's Happening Way Down Deep

My feelings are all in a heap,
I cannot find the words to say, not even a peep.
I want to tell everyone to, "go take a flying leap."

What's happening way down deep

I believe each man who did this to me, is a creep,
They make me sick and I want to weep,
I want to run over them with my jeep.

What's happening way down deep

I know the road ahead to recovery will be steep,
And I do not know if I want to even take this leap,
All I want to do is forget it happened and go back to sleep.

What's happening way down deep

No one hears my signals of distress beep-beep,
Now, I want to stay in the fantasy world of little Bo Peep,
Where someone finds me, like a little lost sheep.

What's happening way down deep

I want a life without the struggles that seem to be knee-deep,
Where everything is not so superficial and skin-deep,
A life I can enjoy with all the positives I can reap.

What's happening way down deep?
I am healing a life, that I want to keep.

—Heather Mesaric

Secondary Healing

$\mathcal{H}$ow To Use The
"Secondary Healing" Section

This section deals with a variety of other areas that I needed to work on to complete my healing process. Some of them may be relevant to you and others not. Since I believe we each have specific fears or weaknesses we want to change, the approach to this section is more individualized. Unlike the first unit where a specific sequence of events was essential to the process, this time you may choose which topic you want to focus on first. Be your own guide. Go at your own pace and after reading the titles of the units, pick those that relate to your personal circumstances.

We all have distinctive needs. You may find that some units don't apply to you or that something else is more useful. Consequently, you may also be surprised to discover that something you thought had no meaning to you, ends up being important as you continue on this journey.

If undesirable feelings continue to re-surface, be patient with yourself and push through whatever comes up. The work itself is bound to open up avenues of thought and is simply another step in the healing process.

The order that the units are presented in this section does not represent the identical sequence that I took. However, the units do incorporate all of the thoughts and feelings I encountered throughout my entire healing process.

The exercises and affirmations will be presented in the same method as in the Primary Healing section. Once again, I highly recommend that you complete them consistently to gain the maximum benefit of their self-empowering messages.

**REMEMBER
TO BE
YOUR OWN
GUIDE...**

**WHILE COMPLETING
THE REST
OF THE BOOK**

In My Bed At Night

While lying in my bed at night,
I wonder whether the fear I feel will ever go away.

While lying in my bed at night,
I am alone with my fears and pain of knowing what will happen.

While lying in my bed at night,
I wonder how long it will be, before he comes into my room.

While lying in my bed at night,
I try to hide and escape into my world of fantasy.

While lying in my bed at night,
I close my eyes and pray, please God keep him away from me.

While lying in my bed at night,
I wonder why no one else sees or hears him doing what he does to me.

While lying in my bed at night,
I know I will wake to discover my nightmares are real, so I will pretend
to be asleep.

While lying in my bed at night,
I cry myself to sleep for fear I will hear the familiar footsteps and hear
the door open.

While lying in my bed at night,
I begin to feel a warm hand lift my nightshirt up, touching me.

While lying in my bed at night,
I stare at the ceiling in order to avoid seeing the truth.

While lying in my bed at night,
I sometimes make plans to escape or hurt the man with the hand.

While lying in my bed at night,
I will lose more of my dignity; I will lose another part of me, because it
will go deep inside me.

While lying in my bed at night,
I will lose all hope that this will ever end.

While lying in my bed at night,
I know this night will be just like the others before, one of fear, anger,
disgust and where…

I lose my right to privacy, sleep and where I have "no voice."

I HATE LYING IN MY BED AT NIGHT.

—Heather Mesaric

*N*ightmares/ Dreams

Nightmares only last as long as we hide from our fears and memories. Once we confront them, asleep or awake; we free ourselves from their hold.

~*Heather Mesaric*

All of us have dreams, and at one time or another, nightmares. However, we survivors tend to have more and they are usually consumed with the pain we are feeling.

You may begin to notice that when you start dealing with the abuse, your dreams become more terrifying and to some extent very real. While it can be frightening, my therapist has assured me that this is very normal and actually healthy. My dreams became so intense I could not believe they were not really happening. I felt myself being touched. I heard the voices of my abusers. I honestly thought my dreams were real. Some nightmares were so chilling that I'd relive the abuse and awake with great anxiety.

My therapist urged me to look at the meaning of the dreams. We discovered that my dreams were helping me to remember situations that were hard for me to face in the waking hours. My sub-conscious was allowing me to recall the past and sort out my feelings and apprehensions. This included a range of emotions from my fear of sexual intimacy, friendships (both male and female), family relationships to the possibility of a recurrence of the abuse.

The characters in my dreams were monsters, scary animals (snakes, wolves, spiders etc.) and strangers. I noticed after a while that my dreams began to show patterns and similarities to the abuse. My therapist showed me how to change the feeling of being a powerless victim even in my dreams. She told me to confront the villains in my dreams and tell them to stop bothering me. I would go to sleep with this thought on my mind and after a few attempts; I was able to face the demons in the night. As I healed, the dreams began to disappear.

Journal Assignment: Start writing about your dreams and create your own dream diary. The best way to do this is have a paper and pen right at your bedside so that you can put the information down as soon as you awaken. Write out everything you can remember about your dreams and/or nightmares trying to find patterns or themes. See if there are any similarities between your dreams and the abuse. Believe it or not, there is a definite connection and once it is discovered it can be resolved and become an important part of your healing process.

Once I uncovered what my patterns were, the players in my dreams became a little more real. I could sense the animal characters were my abusers. I realized I had to confront them and take control over my dream world as I was beginning to do in my everyday waking life. It takes practice and courage. When I dreamed about the devil wanting my soul I would say, "No, you can't have it." With frightening creatures I would try and find out what they wanted from me. To make this work you must prepare yourself <u>before</u> going to sleep. You can think or say these words out loud to help reinforce them in your mind, "No matter what I dream or how I feel in my dream, the dream creatures cannot hurt me. I have the power to make them go away." When you face anything in your dream that alarms you say, "Go away. Get out of my dream." as adamantly as you can. Keep doing this with a firm stand and you will find that the "monsters" in your dreams will go away fairly quickly.

Your Week's Affirmations: These are the ones that I used and found very helpful. For the next week say the following affirmations as often as possible, in order to create new patterns of "positive thinking." Some days I repeated them more than ten times in an hour or whenever I thought about them. My index cards really helped me to keep saying them often. Remember, you can create your own if these do not say what is in your heart.

Day one: I will remember my dreams.
Day two: My dreams cannot hurt me.
Day three: I am not afraid of my dreams.
Day four: I want to remember my dreams.
Day five: I truly believe my dreams cannot hurt me.
Day six: I believe my dreams can and will help me.
Day seven: I know my dreams help me.

In order for this to work you must trust yourself and believe that all the changes you have gone through have given you the strength you need to confront your fears, even while you are dreaming.

Remember: You have control over your life and yes, even your dreams. Dreams can be beneficial by helping us with our pain, anger and fears. The nightmares will decrease as you heal. You will notice, as you take control over your destiny you will be more in control of both the waking and sleeping worlds. You will begin to dream about being in control and being more powerful as time goes by.

*B*oundaries

Limits are made in order to establish standards and expectations for everyone to follow, however, not everyone follows them.

~Heather Mesaric

Every aspect of our lives demands boundaries of some form or another. They define how we interact with others. Unfortunately, abuse survivors lose the ability to maintain or understand normal boundaries required in common situations. By this, I mean that we don't seem to have a sense of limits or to grasp the meaning of invasion of personal space for others and ourselves. For example, we might disclose our personal history too quickly in a relationship. We may touch or stand extremely near to someone and not be aware of the other person's discomfort with our closeness.

Within minutes of starting a conversation with complete strangers, I would find myself telling them my life story. I felt confident divulging very personal information because I felt I wouldn't likely see them again and therefore had nothing to lose. Expecting them to be as proud of my accomplishments as I was, I would relay private details about myself and my healing process. To protect my boundaries (which had never been safe in my childhood), I needed to learn when it was appropriate to reveal my past and to whom.

Dealing with the past made me aware that every boundary had been crossed in my relationships with the male figures in my life. I had to realize that there were no limits in place for me or for them (the abusers) as I was growing up. If there had been, the abuse would not have occurred in the first place.

The biggest challenge for me was to re-learn the normal boundaries expected by society, friends, family and others whom I encountered on a daily basis. It seemed that at times, I was insensitive to the feelings of others. I tended to get too close, touching their shoulder, arm or back without thinking of their preference. It did not occur to me that they might feel I was intrusive.

I also allowed myself to be touched by strangers even when I felt uncomfortable because that had been "normal" to me. More times than I want to remember, I found myself engaging in fondling, heavy kissing and sex within a short time, often within hours of meeting a guy. I did not set any limits for myself or them and never said "no" because I didn't know it was an option. Saying no had never helped in the past so why bother now. Of course, I was hurt and left wondering when the men I met never called back or ignored me when we ran into each other in public. This was very painful for me and even as I wondered if I had done something wrong, I knew deep down they had only wanted sex.

As I healed, I began to say "no" all the time. It was a new way of being and I enjoyed it. I was finally learning that I had control over my body and had a right to decide who could or could not touch me ever again.

I went from one extreme to the other, having sex all the time to no sex at all. Taking a break was such a relief. I began building friendships first and only then taking it further if I really wanted to. It was my choice not theirs.

Another challenge with boundaries for myself and other abuse survivors can be a pattern of being uncommonly wary and protective. We might keep a distance that is awkward or inappropriate for the situation. For example, speaking to a man from a distant position across the room instead of sitting nearby. There were times when I would be so cautious that I would not share anything, especially with the people I cared about. Usually with close friends and family, I kept my feelings and thoughts to myself.

Understanding what was normal and acceptable was not easy for me. I wanted to keep my family and friend relationships on a superficial level to avoid getting too close to anyone. It was a way to prevent myself from becoming dependent or vulnerable. I did not want to experience any more pain and disappointment or be put in situations in which I could not handle the outcome. Having boundaries that are too rigid can prevent us from having love in our lives and the support we need to heal our wounds.

I spent a lot of energy keeping people (especially my immediate family) at a distance. I did not want anyone to see how much I was hurting and how afraid I really was. There was also a sense that if they knew how I was suffering they might pity me. It was a conflict for me because I desperately needed their love and support, but was unable to trust that becoming close could be safe and nurturing.

As I learned to set new boundaries for myself, my self-esteem improved. For the first time in my life, I did not feel like a tramp or cheap slut. I liked myself and could look in the mirror and say, "Good for you." At night, I slept well knowing that I was moving my life in a positive direction.

You may have experienced some of the situations that I have described. If so, start to think of ways that you can set limits and boundaries in your every-day life. This takes time; so, try not to change too many things at once. Changing slowly and being successful is more important than trying to do too much and failing.

Journal Assignment: Write in your journal some of the things you tell people. Who do you tell your most secretive stories to? Is it your loved ones, family, friends, strangers or no one at all? When you talk about these things how do you feel afterwards? Were you glad you talked or were you embarrassed? Did you tell too much? Begin to get in touch with what you tell people and to whom. Do you want to make a change in this area? If so, how and why? Be honest with yourself. List positive ways you can interact with others without going overboard with your personal history.

Journal Assignment—**Exercise Two:** Pay attention to how close you stand to people. Do you find yourself touching others when you talk to them? Do people tend to step away from you when you approach them? Do you have sex on the first date, or do you not date for fear of being touched? Be honest. I know that sometimes it's hard to look at yourself objectively and even more difficult to write it down. Remember no one is going to see your journal unless you want them to, so go ahead and tell the whole truth. Journal writing will help you to discover your true feelings and you will learn so much about yourself. Keep a record of your interactions with others for about a week. If you want, you can ask a friend to be an observer for you and record the distance, the reactions of the person who you encountered and to give you honest feedback. In other words, do whatever you need to do to understand your habits.

Journal Assignment—**Exercise Three:** Write down ways that you can set new boundaries and limits for yourself and with others. How do you want to be treated? What are some ways you can treat others differently? Think of actions that would enable you to feel connected to others, yet, provide the necessary parameters for healthy encounters with people. Be creative, as you look at all the situations you experience in your daily life within your community, your work, and home.

Journal Assignment—**Exercise Four:** Write down the times when you have shut important people out of your life and kept things to yourself. Do you want to tell them something, but can't find the words? Take some time to write what you really want to reveal to those closest to you. Then, sit down face-to-face and talk to them about whatever it is you have been hiding. You could also choose to send them a card with a personal letter that tells your feelings. This is a time for you to open up and thank your supporters, letting them know how much they mean to you. You can express your admiration for their fine qualities and show how much you care. In your journal write, "I deserve to be loved in a nurturing way. I love the people I have chosen to spend my life with. I can show others that I care and love them."

Your Week's Affirmations: These are the ones that I used and found very helpful. For the next week say the following affirmations as often as possible, in order to create new patterns of "positive thinking." Some days I repeated them more than ten times in an hour or whenever I thought about them. My index cards really helped me to keep saying them often. Remember, you can create your own if these do not say what is in your heart.

Day one: I am setting realistic and healthy limits for myself.
Day two: I make good choices with my boundaries.
Day three: I understand and accept my new boundaries.
Day four: My limits and boundaries have a real purpose.
Day five: I am able to set positive limits and boundaries.
Day six: I continue to make good choices and set boundaries for my-self.
Day seven: I enjoy setting new limits and boundaries for myself.

Remember: Learning to interact with others in a new way takes time and practice. Setting limits and boundaries is an ongoing process. It won't happen overnight and you will find that as you continue to heal it will be much easier. Old habits can be hard to change. Be gentle with yourself when you set new goals.

*I*solation

Isolation can occur even when there are others around you, especially when you don't know how to communicate your thoughts, feelings and experiences with them.

~Heather Mesaric

Before my healing process, I spent a lot of time alone. Even in a crowd of people, I had the unique ability to be solitary. I tried to avoid contact with others to prevent the development of any type of serious relationship. Often, I felt I did not know how to carry on a conversation and was worried I'd say the wrong thing or be asked something too personal. I did not want others to know that I was raised in a foster home because of my parents' inability to care for me. I didn't want to find myself divulging more of my story than people would want to hear or that ultimately, I'd be sorry I shared.

A lot of times, I would tune the world out, stand back and just listen, nodding my head in agreement every now and then. This gave the appearance that I was participating in the conversation when I was really not involving myself at all. I felt and acted like an outcast. The majority of the time, I thought of myself as a "fifth wheel" and very out-of-place in social gatherings.

When I began my healing process, I was surprised to find that more than ever I wanted to spend time alone. I would write in my journal, watch television, or do nothing at all. My preference to disassociate from others was based on a feeling of being overwhelmed by the events of my past and wanting to deal with them in private. I could react to the feelings by crying or screaming and not worry about having to talk about it to anyone else unless I wanted to.

Most of the time, I chose to be alone. Going through the healing process allowed emotions to surface that were buried deep inside me. Not always sure how to handle these emotions, I found that staying by myself gave me the opportunity to explore these feelings in a safe environment. Often for me, isolation seemed the only way to cope with my insecurity, anger and despair.

Isolating myself appeared to be a great stepping-stone in my recovery, but I took it to the extreme and began spending too much time alone. Sometimes I would stay in bed for days or find things to do around the house that really didn't need to be done. I would make these meaningless jobs my priority in order to have an excuse not to be around others and avoid answering the phone. I wanted to fade into the woodwork. Isolation became my crutch to avoid dealing with the outside world.

The best way for me to get back into life was to go out and get involved. *I had to force myself to become an active part of the outside world.* I slowly began to attend social functions with family and friends and I tried to develop interests outside my home. These activities included swimming at the local swimming pool, sitting in the park with other mothers while our children played, going window shopping in a mall and talking to the store clerks. I made myself get out of the house just to be around people. I knew I needed to take small steps and stay involved in activities for short periods of time. I knew I needed to create opportunities for meeting new people and learning how to communicate with them. I needed to break the negative pattern I'd been creating so that I didn't become a prisoner in my own life. I involved myself in the outside world in order to continue to heal from the pain and suffering of abuse. As I became more involved with activities and other people, the loneliness and isolation gradually began to fade.

This was not an easy task for me and I had to self-talk my way through it many times. I often found myself saying, "You can talk to this person. Count to ten than ask them something. Go over to them and say something—anything." It could be about the weather, a compliment about their clothing, hair, anything". I would not stop until I made contact with someone in order to start a conversation. I had to force myself out of the house on many occasions and to reassure myself about the reality that even though it was hard, the effort would be well worth the insecurities I was feeling. I kept reminding myself that this was only a phase like all the others that I had overcome and I would get through this one too.

I found that for me, joining organizations and support groups was really helpful. To enhance my career I studied material that developed my skills. I allowed myself to be open to interesting activities that created a new social life for me. As my self-confidence grew, I felt more comfortable engaging in conversations and even became intrigued with the world at large. Reading newspapers, following current events and getting involved with local affairs gave me the ability to participate in discussions without feeling stupid or uninformed.

Please remember that healing from abuse is a form of grieving. You are grieving the loss of your childhood, youth or adulthood. Something precious has been taken away and it's both appropriate and wise to spend some time alone. However, you need to be aware of when you pass a reasonable point and you are the best judge of that. Be sensitive to the idea that you may be withdrawing more than is beneficial for you.

Journal Assignment: Write down the periods of time when you isolate yourself. What percentage of your time are you alone? Why do you isolate yourself? What are your fears, anxieties? *What are you really trying to avoid?* Be honest. Dig deep and think about your answers. Take as long as you want to write in your journal as you discover more truths about yourself.

Journal Assignment—Exercise Two: Ask yourself these questions: "Why do you feel you need to spend so much time alone? What are you accomplishing by isolating yourself?" Look at your answers. Is there a pattern? Do you isolate yourself for the same reason each time?

(Once you have re-established yourself back into society, i.e. spending more time outside your home than inside, re-read this section and reflect on how far you have progressed. Feels great, doesn't it?)

***Journal Assignment*—Exercise Three:** Now list a few friends who you can call on to help you break this cycle. Who do you trust to get you out of this slump? Write down their names and make a point of calling them over the next few days. Discuss your plans to get re-connected with the world and get out and have some fun.

It is very important that you interact with others and do not isolate yourself. Isolating yourself can become an unhealthy pattern that grows more difficult to break with every day that passes. We are social beings, and even though there may be times it seems unlikely, we do thrive on being with other people. To help you regain your position as a fully functioning member of society you need to be involved in activities that interest you.

When I took a close look at why I was avoiding contact with others I discovered a fear of being rejected and not belonging. I made positive changes that helped me become a strong woman who can stand on her own two feet. I am so proud of who I am today. You too can be proud. Take that first step, get out of the house, and start connecting. Other people care about you and will want to help you build a positive experience in the world, if you let them.

Your Week's Affirmations: These are the ones that I used and found very helpful. For the next week say the following affirmations as often as possible, in order to create new patterns of "positive thinking." Some days I repeated them more than ten times in an hour or whenever I thought about them. My index cards really helped me to keep saying them often. Remember, you can create your own if these do not say what is in your heart.

Day one: I am able to be with others without fear.
Day two: I am a positive person to be around.
Day three: I am developing positive skills so I can be with others.
Day four: I have a lot to offer those around me.

Day five: Others learn from me, I have a lot to offer others.
Day six: I am able to share my interests and ideas with others.
Day seven: I am a wonderful person and people love being around me.

Remember: Isolation can provide an opportunity for you to heal the pain and sorrow of your past as you rebuild your life. This takes time and determination on your part. You can be your own best friend if you are honest, take risks and devote your life to the healing process. Think of it as reaching a new milestone every day. You owe it to yourself to start getting involved in the community that you live in. Show the world that you too have a lot to offer. You are unique, special and, most of all, lovable.

C*learing The Closet of The Mind*

When one cleanses the mind, it not only allows one to forgive and forget. It also gives them the opportunity to start over.

~*Heather Mesaric*

There were many times during my healing process that I wanted to throw away the feelings and memories of my past. I wanted to erase them, destroy them or just cut them out of the picture of my life. For me, it was wanting some control over whether I could destroy or keep the memories.

The good news is that I did in fact find a way to eliminate what was not helpful to me and feel wonderfully relieved in the process. It all started one day when I was cleaning out my closet. I began throwing things out that did not fit me anymore, things I did not like, gifts that had sat unopened and so on. My room ended up in a big mess. Clothing, shoes, books, and just plain junk everywhere. There were some real treasures like forgotten trinkets of my youth, an old school portrait, and track and field awards from Elementary and High School. Everything else had no meaning for me and was cluttering up my life.

As I threw out the things, I no longer wanted I noticed I was feeling different inside. As most of us do when sorting through clothes, I found some evoked fond memories while others made me wonder why I wanted them in the first place. As I cleaned, I laughed and cried, throwing out some articles instantly without any attachment. They seemed so easy to discard.

This exercise felt so good I wanted to harness the feeling. I began to wonder whether this would work with my healing process. I decided to try it and it worked like magic.

The first thing I did was sit down and write out a list of the negative thoughts I wanted to get rid of. I was brutally honest. I included statements, feelings of despair, hurtful memories, angry thoughts, accounts of the abuse itself and so much more. It was a reflection of all the anger, frustration, and helplessness I'd felt over the years. I did not hold anything back. I kept writing over several days as I worked towards my goal of discarding everything. I wanted to rid myself of "all that awful stuff" that had been making me miserable. When I could no longer think of anything else to write, I re-read my journal to make sure I hadn't missed anything.

When I was finished, I took the pages and sat down quietly. I took a deep breath and began ripping up the papers and picturing in my mind everything that was being eradicated. As I tore into the sheets, I thought, "Gone, gone for good." I knew that in the future I might recall some of what I wrote, however, they would just be passing thoughts. I re-did the exercise whenever necessary until I felt the "stuff" was gone.

There are other ways you can rid yourself of all the "stuff" that is not helpful to you. Remember that however you choose to dispose of the junk, it should represent throwing out or destroying it. This could include using a paper shredder, burning the pages in a fireplace or cutting them up with scissors. The point is that they are irretrievable when you are finished with them. When the pages have been trashed, remove them from your home as soon as possible. Gather up the pieces or ashes and make sure they get into the next garbage collection or take them to a recycling or landfill site yourself. You do not want these thoughts to linger around your home. Do not keep the contents on your property or anywhere you go any longer than is absolutely necessary. The secret is to dispose of them as quickly as possible. If you have to wait a day or two, you can say, "That's the 'stuff' I no longer want or need." Imagine the refuse in its destroyed form.

My method of choice is handwriting because it requires more energy and focus. If you decide to use a computer be sure that you destroy your work at the end of every session if you do not complete the work all at once. Storing your notes on your hard drive makes it too easy for them to be saved well past their usefulness. The point is to get rid of the negative thoughts, not let them simmer on your system for days at a time.

Journal Assignment: Make a list of all the negative thoughts and self-talk that you want to be rid of. Be very detailed and totally honest about all the things you say or believe about yourself. It's best to set aside a period of time to complete the exercise. However, if it does take more than one session, be careful not to drag it out and keep the negativity alive. When you are sure that you are done, sit still and read over the pages to be certain you have covered everything. Then, begin destroying them by ripping and tearing them into tiny pieces or slowly burning them in a fireplace. As you let them go repeat out loud "Goodbye, you are gone for good."

*Journal Assignment—*Exercise Two: Write in your journal a promise that you will rid yourself of all the negative mind clutter that occurs on a regular basis. Make a commitment and be as specific as you can to make sure you follow through. This could be done daily, weekly, monthly, yearly whatever works for you. I found that when I first started doing this I was doing it weekly, then monthly, and now, I make a point of doing it when I clean my closets on an annual basis. Usually in September when I am putting away summer things to make room for the fall/winter season, I organize my closet. This is the time that I throw out anything around my house that I am not using. I get rid of all the junk, mentally and physically that is no longer needed or wanted. It always feels so refreshing and uplifting when it is completed.

Your Week's Affirmations: These are the ones that I used and found very helpful. For the next week say the following affirmations as often as possible in order to create new patterns of "positive thinking." Some days I repeated them more than ten times in an hour or whenever I thought about them. My index cards really helped me to keep saying them often.

Remember, you can create your own if these do not say what is in your heart.

Day one: I clear my mind with ease and open it to positive thoughts.
Day two: It feels good to nurture my new thoughts about myself.
Day three: I feel good when I think only good thoughts of myself.
Day four: I am only thinking positive thoughts about myself.
Day five: The pleasure of peaceful thoughts occurs often.
Day six: I love the new peaceful thoughts that occur on a daily basis.
Day seven: I love the way I think and feel. I now feel great about myself.

Remember: You can do any of the exercises as often as you need to. You have control over your life and you can choose what is good for you. Decide what "stuff" you want to keep, not only in your surroundings, but in your mind as well. Continue rebuilding your life and give yourself a big hug for working so hard. You deserve it. This task was well worth the effort and just think, the more you throw out those negative thoughts the less you will have. Fill your mind with pleasant memories and stimulating ideas. Nurture yourself everyday as often as you can.

Clothing—Promiscuous Or Cover-up

I don't like dressing this way, but I don't know what else to wear.
~Heather Mesaric

The clothing I wore reflected how I felt about myself during various periods in my life. I am sure that other survivors will relate to one or both of the styles I chose. Without necessarily being conscious of it, our manner of dressing has a voice of its own.

We make a statement about ourselves by the way we dress and at some point every one of us has been judged by our choice of clothing. This can range from complimentary impressions such as attractive, neat and professional to sloppy, skimpy, and distasteful. Whether we like it or not, people will often base their opinion of us on the way we attire ourselves.

I had an extremely negative attitude towards myself and this showed up in my choice of clothing. Either I dressed very promiscuously or I covered up my body completely. During my healing process I began to make changes to my appearance. I knew that I needed to dress in a way that mirrored my new positive self-image to show the world I was proud of who I was becoming. I began asking myself some painful and challenging questions to get in touch with why I dressed as I did. Each time I considered an outfit I asked myself "Will this look appealing, promiscuous or defensive?"

As I became more sensitive to what I was portraying to the world, I made better choices. The impression I'd been creating on an every-day basis was no longer acceptable to me. Now, I cared about how I looked and started taking more time with my appearance as I shifted from a negative to a positive picture.

Journal Assignment: Write in your journal how you dress on most days. What is your style? Do you wear baggy, unattractive clothes, or do you choose revealing, sexy and provocative garments? Write down how your clothes make you feel when you wear them. What is your favourite outfit and why? Get in touch with your attitude towards your appearance. Do you feel good about how you look? Do you care? Would you like to change how you look, and if so why? If not, why not? Are you even aware of why you dress the way you do? Is there a purpose to how you dress?

Your Week's Affirmations: These are the ones that I used and found very helpful. For the next week say the following affirmations as often as possible in order to create new patterns of "positive thinking." Some days I repeated them more than ten times in an hour or whenever I thought about them. My index cards really helped me to keep saying them often. Remember, you can create your own if these do not say what is in your heart.

Day one: I choose clothing that is tasteful and appropriate.
Day two: The clothing I wear speaks very highly of my self-worth.
Day three: I care about how I look and the clothing I wear.
Day four: I care about how I present myself and only wear flattering clothing.
Day five: I love the clothing I choose to wear.
Day six: I look and feel good about the clothing I wear.
Day seven: I choose clothing that is appropriate for each occasion.

The following sections goes deeper into the two styles of clothing, their causes and effects.

Promiscuous Style: I went through a phase where I wore extremely revealing clothing. My idea was "If I have it, flaunt it." My dresses and skirts were so short and tight I could not move. I wore low cut tops that exposed my breasts. Looking back, I know the image I gave was very sleazy. Wearing those clothes brought me a lot of attention, especially from men. The message I was sending was "I'm easy; so, come and get me." There were times when I liked the attention even though I knew it was for all the wrong reasons. I kept setting myself up for failure by attracting men who only wanted sex. They were not interested in me and definitely not in forming any kind of relationship. Feeling that I had nothing more than my body to offer, I took what I could get. My self-esteem continued to be crushed as I marched along on this self-destructive treadmill to nowhere.

During this period, I was overly concerned about my appearance, as I wanted to look as sexy as I could. It's obvious now that I had no self-respect and dressed this way hoping that men would want and need me. Sadly, pleasing men this way was what I'd learned to do best.

The way I dressed was very significant during the time the abuse was taking place. I constantly faced mixed feelings that ranged from liking my look to being disgusted by the clothing I was forced to wear. In some ways, I was an actress and my wardrobe and make-up helped me play the character. I knew what men wanted to see and I didn't disappoint them.

It was a very confusing time in my life. This style of clothing brought me a lot of scrutiny and I felt very grown-up. I learned at a young age what kind of clothes men were attracted to and didn't consider what type of men were drawn to me. My self-esteem was so low, I would do anything to entice looks, comments, and sex which I thought would make me feel good about myself.

I'd also been taught that this was part of how a woman showed a man she loved him. My foster-father had told me that his choosing my clothes, kissing, and fondling me was his way of teaching me how to show love to my future husband. It took a very long time for me to realize that this was not love at all.

Journal Assignment – **Exercise Two:** Write in your journal your feelings about women whose dress makes them look sleazy or overtly sexy. Describe your reactions and judgements including any you have of yourself. Write down your beliefs about how a woman should dress and act. Do you or have you in the past worn revealing and seductive clothing to attract men? How did you feel and how do you feel thinking about it now? Write your own new belief about how you should dress and behave. If it feels right, discuss your findings from this exercise with one of your support system members.

The other style of dressing I went through was a result of my desire to be unnoticed and unattractive.

Cover-up Style: During the years of abuse and especially after I had begun my healing journey I would find myself determined not to physically expose myself. I was tired of the looks and comments, and most of all I was ashamed of my body. I wanted to hide it from myself and from the men who made me feel dirty and cheap. Most of the time I wore clothes that hid my figure. Lots of layered articles and very loose fitting clothing hid me and made me unnoticeable. I loved dressing in oversized jogging pants and large sweatshirts. If I did wear a pair of shorts, I covered up with big baggy tops. I tried not to wear anything revealing or sexy and pulled extra large t-shirts over my swimsuits. I wanted to deny the fact that I was a woman. Being very self-conscious of the risk of exposure, I avoided public places such as pools, gyms, and the beach. I felt embarrassed by my body and I didn't want anyone to see it.

My attempts to appear unattractive were an effort to keep men at a distance and prevent any potential involvement. My body shame made me feel that I didn't deserve a real relationship with anyone. I kept saying to myself, "Who would want me; I'm a dirty slut." This was a time when I repeated these and many other horrible statements to myself, which only deepened my lack of self-worth.

In order to mask my looks, I also began to gain weight in a very unhealthy manner. I wanted to soothe my sad soul and make myself unapproachable. Expansive clothing did not stimulate compliments and confirmed what I knew, that I was unappealing. It was a vicious circle where I fed the feelings with my own actions. The scars of my abuse were so painful it was much easier to become invisible. If I did receive any flattery, I told myself, "They're only saying that to have sex with me." I constantly wondered what the person's true intentions were. I don't think those who have suffered any type of abuse take compliments very well. We tend to be suspicious of other people's motives. These were some of the things, I discovered about myself once I started to address the underlying reasons for my selection of clothing.

Journal Assignment – **Exercise Three:** You may or may not be aware of why you choose the clothes you do. Take an inventory of your wardrobe. Do you own many articles that are extremely large or loose? Are there more sexy or sleazy clothes? Do you have similar feelings of disgust towards your body?

Take a good look at your clothes and see if you own any that are attractive, well-fitted, stylish and tailored?

Do you own any dresses or suits? Does your wardrobe only consist of big baggy clothing? Is your weight interfering with the clothes you wear? Write in your journal why you think you wear the clothing you do. Be honest, and write down the real reasons why you dress this way. Avoid using the excuse that they are comfortable. Attractive clothes can be comfortable and you could save your jogging outfit for walking or jogging!

Journal Assignment—**Exercise Four:** Over the next few days go out and observe people. The best place I have found is a food court in a mall. Sit with a coffee or soda and look at the different styles of clothing that people wear. Write in your journal your thoughts about what you see. Try to look at those who wear attractive, stylish clothes. What do you think of their appearance? Could you wear them, and if so, why haven't you done so? If you don't think they would suit you, why not? Do this several times over the course of a week or two. You must write in your journal after each trip. Note whether your thoughts change each time you address the question "Would you wear these styles?"

Journal Assignment—**Exercise Five:** After a week or so, start window shopping and getting yourself comfortable with the new styles. You can even try them on to see how you look and feel in them. Write in your journal what the experience was like. Also, when trying on some new looks, pay attention to any comments from sales clerks and make a mental note of your reaction to what is said. Write these thoughts in your journal and if your personal feedback is negative, explore why you feel this way.

If you start to buy and wear these new clothes, you may get compliments from friends, family and co-workers. Say *"thank you"* and acknowledge to yourself this new beginning. Enjoy a new and refreshed look that is revealing the changes inside of you. Be proud of your appearance and your body. Write in your journal "I am beautiful, I look and feel wonderful".

Your Week's Affirmations: These are the ones that I used and found very helpful. For the next week say the following affirmations as often as possible in order to create new patterns of "positive thinking." Some days I repeated them more than ten times in an hour or whenever I thought about them. My index cards really helped me to keep saying them often. Remember, you can create your own if these do not say what is in your heart.

Day one: I am beautiful. I love the way I look.
Day two: I have a great body and I love it.
Day three: I love the way my clothes look.
Day four: I dress my body beautifully.
Day five: I love who I am and how I look.
Day six: I love the compliments I am getting about how great I look.
Day seven: I am beautiful inside and out. I love who I am.

Remember: You can complete any of these exercises as often as you need to. Remind yourself, *"The new me deserves to enjoy life and what it has to offer."* Be proud of your appearance and appreciate the joy this new freedom of choice offers you. Experience a style that is attractive and complimentary to you. You deserve the best.

You Didn't Hear Me

I tried to *tell* you I was unhappy, sad and scared,
I tried to *tell* you what was going on and that it was wrong,
And yet, you didn't hear me.

I tried to *ask* you to read between the lines from the riddles I spoke,
I tried to *ask* you to help me in my own special way,
And yet, you didn't hear me.

I tried to *share* my secrets with you through my actions, not my words,
I tried to *share* my nightmares, memories and even my vulnerabilities,
And yet, you didn't hear me.

I *told* you what I needed in order to feel safe,
I *told* you what I needed in order to be taken care of,
And yet, you didn't hear me.

I tried to *tell* you I did not like what was happening to me,
I tried to *tell* you I cried at night before I fell asleep,
And yet, you didn't hear me.

I tried to *ask* you to listen, question the things that were not right,
I tried to *ask* you to be my ally, in order to stop what I could not,
And yet, you didn't hear me.

I tried to *share* my fears and concerns whenever I could,
I tried to *share* the little things to test your ability to hear,
And yet, you didn't hear me.

I *told* you, you were the only one who could help me,
I *told* you the abuse was happening through my behaviour,
And yet, you didn't hear me.

So I ask you, why were you so blind, why couldn't you see that I was
trying to tell you things without words?
Why couldn't you read between the lines?
Why didn't you make me safe and see that what was happening was not
right?

Why did you accept the words of others, what was wrong with my words? So I ask you, Why were you so deaf? *"Why Didn't You Hear Me?"*

PLEASE HEAR ME AND ALL THE OTHER UNKNOWNS WHO CANNOT SPEAK FOR THEMSELVES.

—Heather Mesaric

Why The Secret And
Why It Took So Long To Tell

Wisdom is knowing the truth and telling it, without fear of the outcome.

~Heather Mesaric

Through my actions and behaviours I tried to tell people about the abuse. When I wasn't successful, I withdrew from the world and pretended everything was perfect, not letting anyone know how wrong things were in my home life.

Even though I refused to go places alone with my foster father, I was told I didn't have the right to decide what I could or couldn't do. I tried to make excuses to be away from him. I went to bed as early as 8:30 p.m. throughout my teen years to avoid him. No matter how hard I tried, somehow he always managed to be alone with me. He arranged to teach me to drive after dinner while his wife put their children to bed. While she prepared breakfast, he woke us all up, which meant him reaching under my clothing to touch me. There were so many times he made an effort to "include" me, such as feeding their horses and going for long walks in the early morning. He appeared to be the caring father figure, but in truth, he was a sexual predator. It seemed like he had all the power and I was a puppet doing whatever I was told to do. It felt like I had no control over my life.

When I did voice my dislike of always "being the one who does everything with him" I was told I was over-reacting. I was continuously reminded, "you are being silly and ridiculous and that I should be thankful that he cared so much about me."

I was forever left with the feeling that I was wrong and maybe this was the way a caring family lived. It seemed that I was the one who was flawed and everyone else was okay. I always wondered what the truth was; "Was it right or was it wrong to be treated this way?" I never really knew. I could not trust my feelings and I could not trust anyone else's reactions. I truly felt alone with the predicament I found myself in each and every day.

There are many reasons why we never tell anyone about the abuse. For most of us, it is shame or fear. We are afraid we will not be believed. We sometimes do not believe it ourselves, so how could we possibly think that others would believe us. Sometimes we are afraid for our own safety as well as others. We are afraid that we will be blamed for the abuse. We believe that we must have caused the abuse on some level or that we deserved to be abused by the way that we acted. We tend to take on the burden that somehow we are responsible for the whole terrible ordeal. Thinking that horrible things do not happen to good people we assume that we are "bad." We doubt that the perpetrator is responsible for their actions. This was definitely my experience of abuse.

During my teenage years, I did not tell anyone because I was afraid that people would think I was crazy. Also, I was especially terrified that I'd be taken away from the only family that wanted me. They were not really mine since the C.A.S. (Children's Aid Society) paid them to take me in. I honestly feared that I would be put into a mental institution or a detention centre for troubled teens. I didn't think anyone would believe my side of the story. Feeling as though I had no voice, I felt powerless to change what was happening. Like so many other victims, I did not tell or do anything to stop it. It remained my secret until now.

With each passing episode of abuse, I continued to feel guilt, shame and a sense of hopelessness. I felt I was not a person with feelings, but an object to be used by its owner, for whatever purpose they wanted.

I tried to keep myself safe from the abuse by staying away from home as much as possible. I found that getting involved in sports, the drama club, and community volunteer work kept me out of harm's reach. This technique only worked while I was out of the house and I still had to face the inevitable when I got home.

No one seemed to hear what I hoped my actions would say. I wanted my behaviour to speak for me, to tell everyone that something was not right. The problem was that *no one heard me*. Everyone thought I was going through a rough teenage phase. My grades dropped and my interest in living became non-existent. I dated guys who also had low self-esteem and no plans for the future. Unfortunately, I no longer cared what happened to me.

When things got so out of control that I became desperate, I took an overdose of pills. I was hoping someone would notice how unhappy I was and ask me what was wrong. However, the professionals believed my foster family who said they thought I was "acting out" because I was pregnant. (I wasn't, but this was their justification for my behaviour.) Of course, they were wrong and I never revealed the real reason. No one asked me, so I did not tell. I continued to feel alone with the knowledge that I was being abused and no one could or would stop it.

It infuriated me that my worst fears were in fact true. No one cared enough about me to find out why I was so miserable. I was so shocked that the so-called "professional people" did not take the time to help me feel safe or ask me questions that would lead to the truth. I was begging for help in the only way I knew how and no one came. It felt like no one understood or wanted to see what was *really going on.* I continued to live with the sexual abuse and it seemed no one or nothing could save me or stop it.

I did not tell because I did not feel safe. Believing no one would listen, I did not feel that I would be understood or accepted. I did not have the courage or strength to take this kind of risk without any support. It seemed especially discouraging that "they" (my community, Government, teachers, and counsellors) did not seem to want to know the truth. I did not have the tools to reveal the ugly reality I was living in. It felt as though I was all alone in the world and *there was no one there to tell.*

Journal Assignment: Write out the reasons why it took so long for you to tell about the abuse, or why you still have not shared what happened. It is important to get in touch with why you hold onto the secret and what STOPS you from trusting others or yourself. Write down some of the things you need to have in place for you to tell. Can you make any of these things happen? Do you have a support system as of yet? If not, you need to find one now. You cannot heal alone. You must tell someone.

Journal Assignment – **Exercise Two:** Write in your journal: *I Promise to tell. I promise to talk about the abuse that I've experienced. I will share this secret. I will tell about my abuse.*

Your Week's Affirmations: These are the ones that I used and found very helpful. For the next week say the following affirmations as often as possible in order to create new patterns of "positive thinking." Some days I repeated them more than ten times in an hour or whenever I thought about them. My index cards really helped me to keep saying them often. Remember, you can create your own if these do not say what is in your heart.

Day one: I am safe. I now make myself safe. I am safe.
Day two: I am doing whatever it takes to feel safe.
Day three: I choose to tell about my abuse.
Day four: I trust those around me, I am sharing my story of the abuse.
Day five: I believe in myself; I choose to share my story
Day six: I trust myself; I love myself, and I feel safe.
Day seven: No one can make me do anything I do not want to.

Remember: You are not alone. Times have changed and sexual abuse is far more understood than ever before. There are caring people who can help and you have the strength to find those who will listen to what has or is happening to you. If you do not know anyone personally, call the "help or distress line" in your community. Or, you can ask your Doctor for the names of professionals, groups, agencies, social workers or anyone else who can help you. You must learn to talk about the abuse. **<u>You must tell someone</u>**. Tell your best friend or your spouse; tell anyone who will listen. You can do it. I believe you can tell and I know that once you do ... the healing process will start to take place.

You are worthy and you need to be heard. Begin to trust yourself and believe that you can make positive changes for yourself. You are a loving individual and you can love yourself for who you are. Do not keep this a secret any longer. Let your **voice** be heard. Give yourself a big hug, buy yourself a beautiful rose or special loving memento. Tell yourself ***"You are worthy of being loved."***

Breaking The Silence

I know that speaking about what happened is very important,
But, I'm scared.
I know that if I speak some people will listen and possibly understand,
But, I'm scared.
I know that the pain will not go away, unless I do something,
But, I'm scared.
I know that the journey to recovery is long and unpredictable,
But, I'm scared.

I know that I have the strength to speak out,
But, I'm scared.
I know that I can make an impact on society's views about abuse,
But, I'm scared.
I know that I am not alone, abuse happens to others,
But, I'm scared.
I know that others can help me through this painful experience,
But, I'm scared.

I know that I can trust others; they can help me if I let them,
But, I'm scared.
I know that I have lots of options available, I can speak out,
But, I'm scared.
I know that I have the power to change my life, and help others,
But, I'm scared.
I know that the love I have for myself and others will serve me well,
But, I'm scared.

Listen to me closely; I am scared because the road to recovery is so
new to me.
I sometimes forget that I am a survivor and that I
can do anything, if I put my mind to it.
I'm scared yes, but this is NOT GOING TO STOP ME from moving
forward in my recovery and *it's NOT GOING TO STOP ME FROM
"SPEAKING OUT."*
I can and will tell the world, what it needs to hear about abuse, *even if
I'm scared.*

—Heather Mesaric

Speaking Out

When you find the words that are hidden inside, let them have a voice and speak about them to everyone who will listen.

~Heather Mesaric

Many, many, years later, I spoke up about the abuse when I could no longer take it any more. I wanted it to stop and I wanted to tell someone. I thought I was going crazy. I thought that if I was put away in a psychiatric facility it had to be better than being routinely abused. I went to my family doctor and spent 1 1/2 hours in his office. I cried and told him everything that was happening on a daily basis. He listened as I told him my fears and asked for his help. Without hesitation, the doctor insisted I pack my bags and get out of that house. He said if I needed money, he would give it to me. He assured me that what was happening was not right and that he would help me any way he could. He was the only one who made me feel safe. I told him I would be moving in with a friend in a couple of weeks for my last year of college.

My doctor being a kind and supportive man would not let me leave his office until I made some phone calls to arrange a place to stay other than my foster home. He (and I) did not want me going back there for even one more night. I was able to reach my college roommate and contacted a friend and her husband to help me move. With no questions asked, they came to get me and I left with them that evening. It was the best thing I had ever done for myself. I did not realize it at the time, but that was the night I began to make positive changes. It was the true beginning of my healing process and it unfolded without my conscious knowledge.

One and a half years later, I married my first husband and I tried to tell him what I'd experienced. Unfortunately, he couldn't understand what I was going through. All he saw was my rejection of him because of what someone else had done to me. He wanted to help me, but neither of us knew what to do. It seemed that no matter what we did, my loneliness persisted. I kept coming back to the realization that I would have to help myself and find the answers I needed. My husband could not comprehend why I constantly pushed him away. He did not understand what I needed in order to turn my life around.

For most survivors, speaking about the abuse is even more terrifying than the abuse itself. We tend to play mind games with ourselves by saying, "Who will believe me? Will they blame me? Will I lose my family, friends, job and more?" ***We spend all our energy keeping the "secret."*** We watch what we say and sometimes stay mute for fear of disclosing the unimaginable. Pretending the abuse never happened, we minimize it by convincing ourselves it wasn't that bad. We fool ourselves by thinking it was only a sick dream, or downgrade the affects by saying it doesn't bother me anymore. Lying becomes a way of coping with the reality and we believe that telling would be harder than suffering the actual crime.

For me, admitting I was a sexual abuse survivor was the most horrifying experience I could ever contemplate because I felt alone, truly alone and deeply ashamed.

I believe 30 years ago it was hard for society to hear or talk about abuse. They did not want to deal with this tragedy and the scandal it evoked. Today, abuse is taken much more seriously and victims have more options to help them deal with the outcome. Offenders are dealt with severely and victims are believed. I hope this is because we survivors in general have made society listen to our stories and concerns. We have taken a strong position and stood up for our rights and ourselves. Our voices are compelling as we tell the world that the abuse has to stop. We are helping to make this happen by speaking out. The stories of how our lives were destroyed stir the courage in others to give their accounts. We have begun to make it safe for them to tell their stories.

Speaking out takes a lot of courage. I do hope that **everyone** who has experienced any form of abuse, no matter how trivial you may want to make it, speaks out loudly and clearly. **Abuse is not okay, no matter how it happens. The secret has to be exposed.** We have to protect others and ourselves from this ordeal. If we join together and make society aware of **how often this happens,** the public will be alerted to how it ruins the lives of innocent people. I cannot stress this enough—**we must speak out for any change to take place**. It starts with me; it starts with you; it starts with us. We owe this to ourselves and others who cannot speak for themselves.

I really believe that by speaking out we will make a big difference and create a safer world in the long run. It takes time, understanding, and education. We survivors have the skills and the experience to know what victims are going through. I want you to hold your head up high when you announce to the world, "I am a survivor, and I am going to make a difference in the world for others who have been abused." "I am going to help put a stop to abuse the best way I know how, by speaking up and having a voice. I am going to tell the world what it needs to hear."

Journal Assignment: Write in your journal, two columns, one for **Strengths** and one for **Areas To Work On.** Under the appropriate column list your strengths and the characteristics you possess that make you confident and capable. Then list any areas you feel you need to improve on or skills you want to develop to make yourself more accomplished. Make a list of people you believe will help you make the necessary changes to fulfill your goals. Add to your list some comments on how your specific qualities have helped you be a spokesperson against abuse in the past or could be an asset in the future.

Journal Assignment—Exercise Two: Write down the strengths you think a person needs to make a difference in how sexual abuse is perceived and dealt with. What are the qualities that are needed to help others with their abuse? What would you tell people to help them heal from their abusive situations?

Do you notice that you already have many of the qualities and strengths needed to help others? Yes, you have a voice and it needs to be heard.

Your Week's Affirmations: These are the ones that I used and found very helpful. For the next week say the following affirmations as often as possible in order to create new patterns of "positive thinking." Some days I repeated them more than ten times in an hour or whenever I thought about them. My index cards really helped me to keep saying them often. Remember, you can create your own if these do not say what is in your heart.

Day one: I have the courage and strength to speak out.
Day two: I trust that people will listen to me.
Day three: I am going to change society's views of abuse.
Day four: My speaking out about the abuse will make an impact.
Day five: I have a message to give to the world.
Day six: I am going to let the world know about this tragedy.
Day seven: I love myself—I am able to speak out about abuse.

Remember: You have many strengths you may not have known you possessed. Be proud of yourself. Feel good about who you are and enjoy the loving feeling that is emerging within you. You are truly a wonderful, loving and supportive person. Smile, laugh and enjoy life more. You have earned every joyful moment there is and you deserve happiness and peace.

DON'T BE
AFRAID TO...

SPEAK UP

ABOUT
YOUR
ABUSE

Friendships...

Take time to grow, and mature,
Take the pain and sorrow away,
Take the good with the bad,
Take us for whom we are.

Can start to develop over night,
Can be there when we need them the most,
Can ensure they make each other feel special,
Can always be there, no matter how far apart.

Help the lonely hours go by,
Help us to grow to be the best we can,
Help in their own special way,
Help us to see the light and joy of life.

May develop with our consent,
May show us happiness and contentment,
May happen to anyone, with anyone,
May last a lifetime, if we let them.

Are like treasures to be cherished,
Are able to nurture our wounds and sufferings,
Are respected and honoured,
Are able to tell the truth about themselves.

Will be dependable and rewarding,
Will love for the sake of loving,
Will have an impact on each other,
Will accept our faults, and misconceptions.

Have time to find joy, love and caring,
Have the ability to blend together to form unity,
Have the time to comfort others when you are troubled,
Have plans for the future and support our dreams.

MOST OF ALL: FRIENDSHIPS CAN BE WONDERFUL, LOVING AND GIVING.

—Heather Mesaric

*T*he Importance Of Friends

A true friend can be a blessing, an angel sent from God. We have to be willing to let the person into our lives and heart for the relationship to flourish.

~Heather Mesaric

Most of my growing up years I did not want to get too close to people for fear they would find out about the abuse. I was usually alone and not sure how to make friends or how to keep them. I really felt like a social misfit. My distant, cautious attitude did not allow people to really get to know me. The few companions I had would ask me, "Why are you so quiet?" or "How come you don't get involved with the conversation?" and sadly, "Don't you ever have fun?"

It was not until I became an adult that I realized what friendships were really all about. One female friend taught me a lot and was the only one who accepted me for who I was. In spite of my faults and fears, she stuck by me and helped me discover the wonderful world of friendship. With her guidance, I developed a healthy understanding and acceptance of loving friendships. It was the most beautiful feeling in the world. I might add that this did not happen overnight. I had to work at the relationship and frequently take a close look at who I was and what I wanted from a friend. She helped me lay down the foundation for all the other amazing friendships I have made since.

One of her curious characteristics was that she loved males and talked very highly of them. I would tell her how I hated men and what they did to me. Her favourite saying was ***"They aren't all like that. Most of them are different."*** Of course, I did not believe her and we engaged in some heavy discussions that sometimes led to shouting matches. She would push me to express my anger and resentment towards men. I learned later that this was her way to get me to talk about my pain. Looking back, I released a lot of turmoil and emotion in those heated conversations.

Thanks to my friend, I began to see men in a different light. I realized that I could in fact learn to like men and maybe someday, even fall in love with the right man. She helped me to find the little girl inside and the woman I wanted to be. I learned to be a friend and to unlock the hidden doors deep in my mind.

Building friendships takes time and you need to be willing to take risks. You need to look at how you respond towards others and how they treat you. There are many questions you can ask yourself, to evaluate whether the friendship is a positive one for you or not.

Journal Assignment: Write down what you want in a friend and what your friendships mean to you. What are some of your fears and worries? Would you change anything about your friends and if so, what? Ask yourself questions such as, "Does this person listen to my concerns? Does this person accept me or do they spend all their time trying to change me? Do I feel good when I am with this person or do I feel that there is something wrong with me? Do we plan things together or is this relationship one sided? How important are my friends to me?"

I believe friends are very important and that we all need friends.

Friendships will come and go and when they do dissipate, don't feel guilty or hurt. The reasons may be due partially to the fact that you no longer have the same things in common. You might have grown apart and this is okay for both of you. When it happened to me, I used to blame myself and spend many hours wondering why. I would question myself, looking for mistakes and blaming the break-up on my inadequacy. Now, I no longer torture myself in this manner. I accept that people will move in and out of my life and that's just the way it is. I like to think I give my best in a friendship and I let them go with fond memories. If I find myself missing someone and wondering how they are doing, I send them a loving thought to take care of themselves wherever they are. I honestly believe I give my all in every relationship and that I and the other person both gain from each other.

I do want to point out that there are sometimes occasions when you may feel completely alone. It may seem like the world is against you and you have no friends at all. Perhaps you will go through stages of loneliness and even withdrawal. It is usually during these times that, surprisingly, we push people away. This is when we want and need them more than anything else in the world. During these bouts we may play games with ourselves thinking, "I don't need anyone. I can take care of myself." or "I've managed to be without friends before and I don't need them now." I used to do this all the time. Does this sound familiar to you?

Journal Assignment—**Exercise Two:** Write your thoughts about being lonely. Do you push away people who could be potential friends and if so, why? How can you break this cycle? What could you do to help yourself be more friendly and accepting of others? What do you want in a friend? Make a list and start looking around. Your next-door neighbour may have all these qualities or someone at work might want to be a friend. What is really stopping you from developing meaningful friendships? Be honest. Now ask yourself what you need to do in order to change all this.

Only you can alter this pattern. You can bring yourself back to the positive side of life. It is very easy to blame others for not taking care of our needs; yet, we must remember we now have control over what happens to us. We have the responsibility to take care of ourselves. Love comes from within and only we can validate the love we search for. When we first love ourselves, we can then love others. Learn to be a friend to yourself, treat yourself with kindness, respect, and admiration.

Your Week's Affirmations: These are the ones that I used and found very helpful. For the next week say the following affirmations as often as possible in order to create new patterns of "positive thinking." Some days I repeated them more than ten times in an hour or whenever I thought about them. My index cards really helped me to keep saying them often. Remember, you can create your own if these do not say what is in your heart.

Day one: I am a good friend.
Day two: I have a lot to offer to my friends
Day three: I value my friendships. They are special
Day four: I am able to learn a lot from my friends.
Day five: I show my friends the real me, I am lovable.
Day six: Friendships come easy to me. I am a great person to be around.
Day seven: I love my friends as I love myself.

Remember: In order to be a friend to others we must be a friend to ourselves. We have the ability to reach out to fellow friends and we have a lot to offer them. We are wonderful individuals in spite of having been abused. You deserve to be happy and to have wonderful, caring, loving friendships with others. *Love yourself and love your friends.*

REMEMBER…

YOU

ARE

<u>NOT</u>

ALONE…

The Grief I Feel

I no longer deny myself the pain,
I know I must experience this in order to grow and heal.

I allow myself to go through the doors that were once closed,
In order to find the secrets that are locked away inside me.

I know this journey will not be easy and at times,
I will want to run and hide,
Instead, I'll open my heart to let the love come rushing out.

I will make sure that I use the support I have from my friends,
therapists, and loved ones,
I know I cannot take this journey alone.

I release my over crowded feelings of despair from my mind,
I welcome the uncertain feelings of excitement and anticipation.

I used to blame others and myself for the abuse,
I now know there is no reason for the blame.

I wanted to trade my life with someone else,
I know that I cannot be anyone but who I am.

I lost my understanding of what it is like to believe in a higher power,
I look inside myself to find the answers, which I know I hold in me.

I no longer have to numb the pleasures of what life has to offer,
I release my fear and allow myself to experience the wonders of life.

I grieve my past,
In order to make room for my new beginnings.

Through my tears of sadness,
I am able to see pools of joy.

Through my struggles with grief,
I still am able to envision that there is hope

—Heather Mesaric

*A*llowing *Yourself To Grieve*

When we grieve the pain away, it leaves room for the joy to enter our heart in a loving way.

~*Heather Mesaric*

There is no question that I had many reasons to grieve. I knew what I had lost over the course of my life. My childhood, my innocence, my self-esteem, my ability to trust anyone and my sense of feeling safe had all been stolen from me. I lost all this and so much more growing up in an abusive environment. I knew I could not bring back what was taken away any more than I could bring back someone who died.

The only way to rid myself of the grief was to get in touch with the sad and angry feelings I had surrounding my loss. As a child, I had wanted to be loved and taken care of in a nurturing way. I wanted the adults around me to have patience and understanding and give me positive attention and happy childhood memories. Yet, all I seemed to get was hate, abuse, shame, denial, secrecy, blame, and confusion. I lost my early and adolescent years, my mother, my father and all the other parental caregivers whom I could trust and learn from. What I gained was a lifetime of being fearful, angry, depressed and most of all *silent*. I was silent so that no one would discover the horrible secrets I was concealing.

The grief I felt was for so many things, like lost dreams and plans for how my life was going to turn out. I knew I never wanted to go through an experience like that again. I grieved for my adolescence and the chance to enjoy learning about the world through innocent eyes. I lamented the lost opportunity to experience the joys of living without oppressive control and bizarre adult behaviours. For example, as a teenager, I never wore normal clothing like other teens, but had to don sexually degrading attire. I was never allowed to talk on the phone with friends as all teenagers do. I did what I was told and never had the right to have a say in my life. I grieved for the imprisoned fun-loving person I knew was locked away inside my frightened shell. To this day, the events and memories of the past occasionally haunt me and I give myself the permission to grieve one more time.

Giving yourself permission to grieve is a great healing process. I still have to push myself through some hard times and remind myself not to be so rigid and solemn. I have to remember that I lost something precious that can never be replaced. Letting myself feel the sorrow and hurt is important to my healing so I can go on with my life. Otherwise, I'd be stuck in the past without any escape. This process can be difficult, but it is critical to letting go and being free.

Grieving is helpful as long as you don't let it control your thoughts for long periods of time. Face the feelings that surface and deal with each as it comes along. Anger does not serve you if you take it out on yourself or someone else. Denial does not serve you if you prevent yourself from remembering the truth. You need to bring these feelings to light so you can rid yourself of their harmful effects on other people and yourself.

Journal Assignment: Write in your journal what you feel you lost during and after the abuse took place. Refer to your childhood or write about what life is like now. The importance of this exercise is to get in touch with the loss you have experienced and the grief you feel for what might have been. Keep writing until you have let it all out and give yourself a few days to complete this assignment if you need to. If you want to cry or be angry, that's okay. Express your grief and, if it feels right, allow someone to listen and comfort you.

Journal Assignment—Exercise Two: When you have written everything you feel you need to write, close your eyes, take a deep breath and sit quietly for a moment. Now, with deliberate movements, rip up the pages and repeat, "I no longer need to grieve my past. I let go of all this hurt and sadness. I let go of my fears, my shame, embarrassment, and most of all, my hate."

Journal Assignment—**Exercise Three:** Write in your journal ***"I let go of my past to make room for new beginnings. I love who I am and I will take care of myself. I love myself."*** Now, write your own affirmation of how you will change your way of thinking. Create an affirmation welcoming your new way of feeling and new way of living. Re-write any of these statements that you find yourself feeling strongly about.

Your Week's Affirmations: These are the ones that I used and found very helpful. For the next week say the following affirmations as often as possible in order to create new patterns of "positive thinking." Some days I repeated them more than ten times in an hour or whenever I thought about them. My index cards really helped me to keep saying them often. Remember, you can create your own if these do not say what is in your heart.

Day one: I allow myself the opportunity to grieve my losses.
Day two: The past is gone; I am able to start a new beginning.
Day three: I welcome my new life with an open mind and heart.
Day four: My new life starts today. It starts right now at this moment.
Day five: I know I am healing my life, by letting go.
Day six: I trust myself totally; I now let go of the past.
Day seven: I make room in my life for new beginnings.

Remember: Grieving is a powerful way to let go of the things that hurt. It is a process, which allows deep healing of the body, soul and mind. Let this process work for you. You lost a lot and can gain so much more by letting go of this hurt. Give yourself the opportunity to feel the pleasures of life.

Personal Healing

*H*ow To Use The
"*Personal Healing*" Section

This section deals with you becoming more aware of your own needs and desires on a more intimate level. Some of you may find the work interesting while others feel it is somewhat provocative or difficult to navigate.

Even though I designed the exercises, there were times I had to stop and deal with the negative feelings that arose. You know your limits and comfort level. Do what feels right for you and skip this entire section if you are not ready. You can always come back to it after finishing the book.

This is your healing process so you can choose what you want to do. My book is only a tool to help you discover your own path for healing from abuse.

Please do not feel you have to complete the exercises in this unit. They are what worked for me and are meant to be guidelines to help you move forward. Be your own navigator. If something doesn't feel right you can change what you need to in order to fit your personality and comfort level.

$\mathcal{P}$ampering Yourself

You deserve to be treated with kindness, love and devotion. What better way to have all of this than by giving it to yourself. After all, you know what pleases you. Treat yourself in ways that only you can appreciate.

~Heather Mesaric

Throughout my life, I had spent a lot of energy and time doing things for others and very little for myself. It was easy for me to look after other people's needs while ignoring my own. I was unable to nurture myself or even take time to make myself feel special in any way. I believed anything I did should be for other people's enjoyment not my own.

I felt strongly that I needed to change this way of thinking and put my own desires ahead of others. Realizing I would have to look at life differently, I started taking time for myself and finding ways to pamper *me*. I began asking myself, "What makes me happy?" and "What could I do to make myself feel special?" One of the best ways I personally found to indulge myself was through aesthetics and creative outlets. I began visiting my hairdresser more often, doing my nails, buying plants, and going to craft stores to window shop. Between the cosmetic treats and browsing through shops, I really began enjoying the time with myself and started to feel like a million dollars.

Spending time alone with a purpose is different than isolating yourself. Isolation is born of a desire to avoid people based on fears and anxieties. Creating special time for yourself allows you to gratify yourself with little things that are important to your well-being. It is a wonderful gift you can give to yourself and I have come to really enjoy my time on my own.

The things I choose to do includes long baths by candlelight, reading a good book, going for walks, visiting an art gallery, sewing clothing for myself, meditating, window shopping, listening to music and sometimes watching a TV special that interests me. I do things that bring me contentment and joy. I am now a strong believer in self-nurturing to give myself love, friendship and respect.

During my youth I did a lot of things I didn't want to do and now I felt it was my turn to make my own decisions. I knew I was no longer at the mercy of society, my work, my family or my friends. If I felt I needed to change jobs, I did. If I had to tell my family I did not like something that was happening, I told them. I began taking care of my needs first so that I would have something to give to others. If it felt right to give up something for someone else, I did so of my own free will. Finally, I had learned the difference between doing something for someone because you have to and doing something because you wanted to.

I truly believe that if you cannot love yourself, you will be unable to love other people including your family, friends and others who are closest to you. It starts with loving your inner child who is still waiting for the unconditional love of someone else. You need to nurture that child and satisfy their longings. Learn to be more caring, kind and generous with yourself. Buy the dress, shoes, perfume, or whatever else you have been waiting for. Buy it without any feelings of guilt, knowing you deserve to be as well treated as anyone else that you love.

Journal Assignment: Write the answers to these questions: "What would make me happy?" "What things could I do to make myself feel special?" If you cannot think of ways to pamper yourself then spend this time writing a list of reasons why you do not think you deserve to be nurtured this way. Find out why you discredit yourself. Read each statement out loud and after each one say, "I deserve to love and pamper myself." Explore ideas and hobbies that interest you. Write these down. Make a list of things that you think would be a lot of fun and make you happy.

Journal Assignment—**Exercise Two:** Start a schedule of pampering yourself for a minimum of 20-30 minutes each day, working up to at least 45 minutes or more. Remember: this is your time, so take the phone off the hook; ask your family to give you privacy, and avoid any distractions that may come up. Within a few days, everyone will adjust to your new regime. Do not do anything for anyone else during this time and make sure what you choose to do is different from your everyday routine. Be resourceful in selecting activities and resist doing chores such as laundry, meal preparation or house cleaning.

Journal Assignment—**Exercise Three:** During your pampering time, think of all the positive things that you have done and continue to do for yourself. Get in touch with your loving emotions and only think good thoughts. This is your time to validate your strengths and reinforce your best qualities. Don't allow anything negative to enter your mind or focus on things you "should" be doing. Relax and enjoy yourself. Believe it or not, 30 minutes will pass quickly and you deserve at least this much time for yourself. You need to love yourself and you are showing this love through the gift of time. Remember that you cannot love or respect others unless you exercise your capacity to love yourself.

I firmly believe we all need to spend some time every day making ourselves feel good. Self-acknowledgement is empowering. I make sure that my pampering time is sacred. No one is allowed to disturb me. When I tell my family, "I'm going to spend the next hour alone" they respect my boundaries and don't interrupt. If you have young children, you may have to make use of their naps or bedtime to create your quiet space. When my children were small, I made the time for myself even if I felt exhausted because I valued the results of the self-care.

With intentional planning, you will find ways to fit some pampering into your schedule. Please make the time for yourself. It is well worth the effort and you will learn to enjoy these moments of personal pleasure.

Your Week's Affirmations: These are the ones that I used and found very helpful. For the next week say the following affirmations as often as possible in order to create new patterns of "positive thinking." Some days I repeated them more than ten times in an hour or whenever I thought about them. My index cards really helped me to keep saying them often. Remember, you can create your own if these do not say what is in your heart.

Day one: I now allow time for myself.
Day two: I deserve to spend time on myself.
Day three: I love to pamper myself each and every day.
Day four: I make time to pamper myself. I deserve it.
Day five: I love myself and I love being kind to myself.
Day six: I give myself all the love I can. I am special in every way.
Day seven: I deserve to be loved and I feel great.

Remember: You are special and are entitled to the royal treatment. You are the only one who can give your inner child the love it deserves and needs. Enjoy your time of pampering. Learn to give yourself what you want.

*R*eleasing Stress And Relaxing

Stress drains the mind, body and soul, while relaxing brings back the life that was once lost.

~Heather Mesaric

There was a time when I was frequently very tense and on edge. I did not know how to relax and had no concept of the healing effects of positive thinking and relaxation.

Every day we experience many stressful situations that can create headaches, stomach upsets, and a sense of being unbalanced. There are many courses that offer alternatives to stress including Yoga, Tai Chi, Meditation, etc. I tried going to formal gyms and exercise classes, but I found it challenging to relax around a lot of other people. I spoke to friends of mine who worked out and asked them to show me what I could do at home. After many hours of trial and error, soreness and laughter, I came up with some relaxation exercises that worked for me. Feel free to make any adjustment you find will help you customize your relaxation program.

Journal Assignment: When you feel stressed make a fist, tense your body, and maintain that state, for as long as you can. Now, release the tension. Visualize the tension leaving your body. Think pleasurable thoughts. I close my eyes and imagine being a flower in the spring. I start with being a bud closed tight (holding onto the tension in my body) and then I slowly open up into a beautiful flower (releasing the tension from my body). I imagine the feeling of the heat of the sun shining on me and a warm breeze blowing around me. I remember the joy of watching the spring flowers come to life after the dead of winter. I welcome this feeling of peace and tranquility. Do this exercise as often as needed during the day. It only takes a few minutes and the results are well worth it.

Journal Assignment—**Exercise Two:** Create a scene in your mind that you think is relaxing. Write out as many details about your setting as possible. Picture it in your mind and write down the particulars of the scene so it is very clear in your mind's eye. As you write, include all of your surroundings such as the leaves on the trees, the feeling of the sun, any breezes, the sound of a river flowing or waves against a shoreline. Keep visualizing your image until you can see it with your eyes closed. Practice being in this relaxing space until you have mastered the technique of stepping into its serenity when a stressful situation threatens your sense of well-being.

If you have any difficulty with your visualization, you may find doing a week of the following affirmations helpful.

Your Week's Affirmations: These are the ones that I used and found very helpful. For the next week say the following affirmations as often as possible in order to create new patterns of "positive thinking." Some days I repeated them more than ten times in an hour or whenever I thought about them. My index cards really helped me to keep saying them often. Remember, you can create your own if these do not say what is in your heart.

Day one: I am able to relax my body when I need to.
Day two: I am able to release any tension that comes up.
Day three: I enjoy allowing myself the pleasures of relaxation.
Day four: I love the feeling of being relaxed.
Day five: I know how to release the tensions in my body.
Day six: I use my relaxation exercises when needed.
Day seven: I love myself and I love taking care of myself.

Journal Assignment—Exercise Three: This is a good exercise when you lie down in bed at night and also it can work in a sitting position on a chair, bus or subway during the day. Close your eyes and concentrate on each body part as you tighten every muscle. Start with your toes and tighten the muscles all the way up to the top of your head. Now imagine the sun shining over you and feel its heat warming your entire body. Begin releasing the muscles in your toes and picture a magic wand gliding over them to relax them. Then slowly move the imaginary wand up over your ankles, calves, knees, thighs, hips, groin area, stomach, hands, lower arms, elbows and, finally your chest. Stop for a moment over your heart and allow the love you feel for yourself and others to flow through you and out. Visualize giving love to everyone around you. Picture yourself in a beautiful, peaceful place and feel the sun continuing to warm your body.

When you have stayed in this place and eased more tension, move the wand up to your shoulders, neck, jaw, mouth, nose, ears, eyes, forehead and up over your head. With each movement, you release the tensed muscle and relax your body. At this stage, allow yourself to see only beauty, hear gentle waves and feel the warmth of the midday sun. Feel how relaxing it is and feel the love that the natural world has for you. Let yourself stay in this stillness for 5 to 10 minutes to completely let go of all stress and tension.

Journal Assignment—Exercise Four: While taking a bath or shower, visualize all the negative feelings, tensions, etc. being washed from your body. Imagine the water is a magnet collecting all the negative energy, leaving you with only positive thoughts and feelings. Then visualize all this negativity going down the drain with the bath or shower water. You can also pretend that the soap is a magnet as you smooth it over your skin. Feel the negative energy being pulled away from your body and watch all the stress disappear as you rinse off. You will feel clean and refreshed with relaxed sensations. Sun and water are natural healers and essential to life. They can help keep you in a healthy and happy state of mind.

***Y**our Week's Affirmations:* These are the ones that I used and found very helpful. For the next week say the following affirmations as often as possible in order to create new patterns of "positive thinking." Some days I repeated them more than ten times in an hour or whenever I thought about them. My index cards really helped me to keep saying them often. Remember, you can create your own if these do not say what is in your heart.

Day one: I relax my body every day.
Day two: I am now aware of when I should relax.
Day three: Relaxing is enjoyable, and keeps me healthy.
Day four: I love myself. I love to relax. I love being relaxed.
Day five: I continue to allow myself the pleasure of relaxing.
Day six: I care about myself; I learn new ways to relax my mind and body.
Day seven: When I relax, I let go. I feel wonderful when I am relaxed.

***R**emember:* Relaxing is a skill and may take time to master. Do not be too hard on yourself if you have to try some of the exercises a few times to get good results. Keep working through them and they will become part of your daily life. You will be able to relax and get yourself through any obstacles you face.

FIND THE

TIME TO

RELAX YOUR...

MIND AND BODY

Loving Myself

Looking in the mirror, who could it be,
Oh yeah, it is me.

The tears of sadness left on the floor, who could it be,
Oh yeah, it is me.

Hearing the inner child's voice, who could it be,
Oh yeah, it is me.

The loud voice I hear screaming, who could it be,
Oh yeah, it is me.

The shadow that is following me, who could it be,
Oh yeah, it is me.

Wearing all those fancy clothes, who could it be,
Oh yeah, it is me.

The sounds of laughter and joy, who could it be,
Oh yeah, it is me.

The beautiful smile on a face, who could it be,
Oh yeah, it is me.

The woman so perfect and free, who could it be,
Oh yeah, it is me.

I could wish, that the things in my life did not happen
However, the person they happened to would not eventually become me.
Therefore, I will continue to look in the mirror and say
Oh yeah, **<u>it is me</u>**.

—Heather Mesaric

*L*ooking At Your Mirror Image

The person we see in the mirror may not be the person we want to see.
We have to be willing to look at ourselves with loving eyes in order to
see our true loving self.

~Heather Mesaric

The person we look at in the mirror reflects not just our physical image,
but also our personal appraisal of our image. Most of us tend to view
ourselves with critical eyes, thinking things such as "I look ugly. I'm fat.
My nose is too big. I'm not tall enough. My hips are too big. My legs are
so fat," etc.

Our image of what we should look like is projected to us through
magazines, TV, advertising, billboards and the entertainment stars in the
movie theatres. The media has all the tools to portray perfect-looking
people. We forget that the people we see go through a rigorous process
to look "naturally beautiful." In some cases, body doubles are even used
when someone doesn't have the particular asset to give the appearance
of perfection.

With illusion, computer images, air brushing, photo enhancements
and more, any man or woman can look flawless in spite of their real
life imperfections. One great looking picture could be the result of hair,
face, legs, arms etc. from more than five different real people. Someone I
know had her "perfect" hands photographed for several advertisements
that used these pictures on a variety of models.

We have to be very careful not to think that we can and should look like the people we see in the world around us. Some people are indeed born with beautiful skin and attractive features. However, most of the images we are bombarded with are those that have been altered to give the impression of perfection.

I believe we all have flaws, yet we are also beautiful if only we would allow ourselves the chance to believe it. Our beauty may be in some body attribute or in the talents we have to share. It may be our strength of character or our unique ability to perform some special task. Learning to accept and cherish who we are will help us to appreciate that we are as unique as every flower, bird, or tree. Some people do suffer with diseases or addictions that cause obesity and other eating disorders which can seriously alter their appearance. These often put them at risk for heart attacks, strokes, diabetes, anorexia etc. and if you fall into this category, you must seek medical assistance to bring your body back to a healthier state. Other people may have challenges with skin conditions, malformations or any number of medical circumstances that affect the appearance of their body. We all have something that isn't quite right and it's what we tell ourselves about our particular situation that can be healing or hurtful.

The hardest part for me was *accepting all* my so-called body faults. I didn't like any part of my body. I hated my hair, my legs were too skinny, my feet too bony, my nails too short (from biting them), my breasts too large, etc. The negative self-talk made it difficult to love my body and the image that others saw. My children would tell me how beautiful I looked and I received compliments from co-workers. I found it very hard to believe what others were saying and to convince myself that I was beautiful.

With a view to changing this self-image, I spent hours in front of a mirror telling myself that I had great hair, pretty eyes, a nice nose and mouth and soft skin. Slowly, I began to like my face. With time, I could look in the mirror and smile at myself. As I got in touch with my inner beauty, I began seeing my reflection in a different way. Once I learned to like this new face, I moved on to standing in front of a full-length mirror and taking in the wonder of my entire body.

Accepting that I was not perfect, but still beautiful was a big step for me. I embraced the woman I saw in the mirror and even permitted myself to embrace the notion that I was extraordinary in every imaginable way. I started liking who I was unconditionally and rejoiced in all the fine feminine qualities that I possessed.

Journal Assignment: Write in your journal all the positive qualities that you know you have. Holding a hand mirror, study your hair, face, skin, eyes and so on. Take a good look and then list all the beautiful qualities you see. Be liberal in your judgements and give yourself fair consideration. For example, if you don't like your eye colour, perhaps you can appreciate the shape and size of your eyes. Do these exercises every day until you can look in the mirror and list at least five positive things about yourself. You can use a small mirror at first, but eventually you must progress to a full-length one. When you do this, try standing naked and if it's difficult at first, gradually uncover your body until you are ready to see it in its most glorious state. (It took quite some time for me to do this, as I was ashamed and disgusted by what I saw. I had to get over the feeling that nudity was bad and that my body was just a sex object for men.)

While looking in the mirror search for the positive and radiant attributes you possess. Learn to appreciate your body and embrace an "I'm okay" attitude. Remember! No negative comments! This exercise may be hard if you tend to put yourself down. Stick with it and you'll stop seeing only flaws and start seeing a lot more charm.

Journal Assignment—Exercise Two: Write in your journal positive impressions about the person you saw in the mirror. What do you like about the image you saw? Write your feelings, comments, and the things you enjoy about yourself. Remember, no negative statements. You are who you are; you need to learn to love yourself. Change will only happen if you really want it to and if you deliberately plan for it in a caring and supportive manner. If you decide to make changes to your body, make them for healthy reasons and don't base them on unreachable standards of perfection.

Your *Week's Affirmations:* These are the ones that I used and found very helpful. For the next week say the following affirmations as often as possible in order to create new patterns of "positive thinking." Some days I repeated them more than ten times in an hour or whenever I thought about them. My index cards really helped me to keep saying them often. Remember, you can create your own if these do not say what is in your heart.

Day one: I love my body, I love my body.
Day two: I appreciate my body. I have a wonderful body.
Day three: I have a beautiful body.
Day four: I love how I look, when I look in the mirror.
Day five: I believe I look beautiful.
Day six: I see myself as beautiful.
Day seven: I love the way I look, and feel about myself.

Remember: Beauty comes from within. We all have to learn to love ourselves for who we are at any given moment physically and emotionally. This is a concept all human beings have to face and not just survivors of abuse. The media destroys the beauty of being plain, tall, or slightly overweight. They continue to portray an image that is not only unrealistic to achieve, but also unhealthy. I truly hope you find a way to remember that you are beautiful just the way you are. We all have unique and wonderful characteristics that are special to each and every individual. I want you to find yours. Cherish those wonderful traits that you alone possess.

Y*our Feelings Toward Men*

Past feelings, hurts and ideas are not carved in stone. These feelings can be changed. The quality of any relationship can be formed into something more precious with the right attitude and approach.

~Heather Mesaric

It has taken a lot of hard work and soul-searching for me to accept men into my life. I used to hate being in the same room with any man. My heart would race, I could not breathe and I broke into cold sweats feeling clammy and nervous. I feared being by myself in elevators, seeing male doctors and dentists or being alone anywhere with a man. I was really terrified that I would be approached or worse, be touched by one of them. In all my workplaces, I was extremely lucky to have only female supervisors. It was a relief to not put my job in jeopardy because of anxieties over sexual harassment.

It was very difficult for me to really connect with my first husband or allow him to get close to me. I felt any gestures he made were an attempt to initiate sex. Resisting his demonstrations of true affection, I would not even allow him to comfort me in a normal way. I pushed him away all the time and caused fights to avoid being near him. Every time he touched me, I flashed back to the abuse.

It was a confusing period for me because I believed that to be loved you had to give sex whether you wanted it or not. Many nights were spent crying because I felt dirty, alone and, most of all, guilty. I could not feel the love I was supposed to feel towards him or allow him to touch me tenderly. It was impossible to foster a normal relationship when I would not allow any good feeling to emerge. Not knowing what was expected of me, I kept my feelings inside and was unable to tell him how I really felt.

Once I came to terms with my resentments towards men, I was finally able to enjoy their company. Some of my closest friends are now males.

Journal Assignment: Write in your journal some of the things you do to sabotage your relationship(s) with men. How do you stay distant from men? How would you like to be with the men in your life? Be honest here. Would you like to be closer? How do you want them to understand and treat you? Make a list of what the perfect man in your life would be like. Include all the qualities you dream of for your ideal partner. Make this a list of all the things you want and need from a devoted partner.

When I did my list after separating from my first husband, I wrote out all the specifics I wanted in a man. To my amazement, my second husband fits the description to a tee. When it turned up in some old files after we were married, I read the list to him. He was totally surprised at the similarities he shared with my "perfect" man.

You can have a wonderful relationship with men and learn to be loved in return. When you are making your list be as particular as you can. My list included: likes children, understands a woman who has been abused, kind, fun, has a beard, smart and so on. I kept writing all the things that I thought would make me happy. I believed that I could find my dream man, and several months later, I did.

Your Week's Affirmations: These are the ones that I used and found very helpful. For the next week say the following affirmations as often as possible in order to create new patterns of "positive thinking." Some days I repeated them more than ten times in an hour or whenever I thought about them. My index cards really helped me to keep saying them often. Remember, you can create your own if these do not say what is in your heart.

Day one: I have a loving attitude about the men in my life.
Day two: Men are special and loving towards me.
Day three: I believe men are great friends and lovers.
Day four: Many men are wonderful and deserve my trust.
Day five: I have new feelings about men. Many are wonderful.
Day six: The men in my life care about my feelings and me.
Day seven: I trust the men in my life. They make me feel safe.

Remember: Not all men want to abuse and hurt you. There are a lot of extraordinary men out there who would like a chance to prove that they love, honour and respect you. Men are special friends and if you give them a chance, they will show they deserve your love and admiration.

Understanding And Accepting Sex In Your Life By Learning To Appreciate The Female And Male Genders

One needs to be accepting of oneself before they can be accepting of others. Only when one has a true sense of themselves can they venture into the unknown world of understanding someone else.

~Heather Mesaric

Talking or even thinking about the subject of sex was taboo for me. I thought of "sex" as a dirty word. When it came to mind or I heard the word I would think vulgar thoughts and was embarrassed by the whole topic. My experience has been that most people prefer not to talk about their thoughts and feelings regarding sex.

All that I knew of sex was learned through selfish men who only cared about their own needs and desires. I did not see sex as something intimate and loving. I was robbed of the experience that sex could be pleasurable for both parties when shared between two loving people.

This prompted me to look at the differences between women and men and come to an understanding of each gender. I believed this would help me to accept sex as a natural and healthy experience in any hetero-sexual relationship.

I decided to explore my thoughts and feelings about my own sexual identity, that of being a woman. Up to this point in my life, I had no model for how a woman could or should participate in a loving relationship. With many misconceptions of what sex meant, I decided to explore the anger I felt around the whole issue. I was curious to learn how a man should treat a woman and I wanted to clarify my own thoughts on how I wanted to experience sex in my life.

To begin to appreciate sex, I knew I would first need to look at how I felt about being a woman. With so many distorted impressions from my past, I wanted to learn to appreciate being a woman and to embrace all the wonderful things that go with it. I also wanted to be very clear on how I truly felt about men and resolve some of the negative attitudes that stood in the way of my having a healthy sexual relationship.

Many questions began to surface as I started the process of examining the differences between men and women. What did I really think about being a woman? What were my deepest feelings about men? What kind of woman was I? Was this the way I wanted to be? How could I change some of my old-fashioned beliefs of what a woman is supposed to be like or how one should behave? Did I like anything about men, and if so, what and why?

Please **note:** that the examples I give in the next few assignments are not meant to imply that either gender cannot possess the fine qualities or attributes of the other. These examples are here to give you an idea of how to get started in making your own lists.

"Your Thoughts About Women"

Journal Assignment: Write your thoughts about women in general. This exercise is to get in touch with your views on women and what you think of them. What are your feelings about women? Do you think they are they weak, strong, loving, caring, hurtful, mean?

Journal Assignment—Exercise Two: Now write in your journal your thoughts on being a woman. Do you like yourself the way you are? If so, why? If not, why not? What are your feelings about being a woman? If you could change anything about yourself, what would it be, and why?

Journal Assignment—Exercise Three: Now write only positive things you associate with women. For example, women can wear pretty dresses, sweet-scented perfumes and flattering makeup. Consider feminine characteristics such as compassion and intuition. List all the things you like that are characteristic of women in general whether or not they are representative of you personally. The main point of this exercise is to list all the positive qualities that you admire in women.

Your Week's Affirmations: These are the ones that I used and found very helpful. For the next week say the following affirmations as often as possible in order to create new patterns of "positive thinking." Some days, I repeated them more than ten times in an hour or whenever I thought about them. My index cards really helped me to keep saying them often. Remember, you can create your own if these do not say what is in your heart.

Day one: I enjoy learning to explore my thoughts on being a woman.
Day two: I am at peace with myself and cherish being a woman.
Day three: I have many wonderful female qualities.
Day four: I enjoy being a woman.
Day five: Being a woman brings me happiness and satisfaction.
Day six: I welcome the new life I give myself as a woman.
Day seven: I love being a woman.

"Your Thoughts About Men"

Journal Assignment: Write in your journal your thoughts about men. Do you like men? If so, why, and if not, why not? If you could change them, what would you change? Be honest with your answers and give yourself time to explore your true feelings.

Journal Assignment—Exercise Two: Now list what you perceive to be the benefits of being male and the attributes of being male such as the wearing of flat shoes, the ability to grow beards and the possession of bodily strength. List the non-physical qualities of males that come to mind such as leadership ability, a sense of responsibility, etc. Add all the things you like about men in general whether or not they are representative of the men closest to you. The main point of this exercise is to list all the positive qualities that you admire in men.

Your Week's Affirmations: These are the ones that I used and found very helpful. For the next week say the following affirmations as often as possible in order to create new patterns of "positive thinking." Some days I repeated them more than ten times in an hour or whenever I thought about them. My index cards really helped me to keep saying them often. Remember, you can create your own if these do not say what is in your heart.

Day one: I accept and appreciate men.
Day two: I see love and tenderness in men.
Day three: I love being around men in my home and community.
Day four: I admire the many wonderful qualities men have.
Day five: I love and cherish the men in my life.
Day six: Men are loving and caring and I enjoy being with them.
Day seven: My feelings about men bring joyful experiences.

Journal Assignment—Exercise Three: After completing at least one week with the above affirmations write your thought on men now. Is there a difference? Can you see positive qualities that you were unable to see before. Repeat the affirmations as often as you feel is necessary to fully embrace the positive feelings towards the men in your life and community.

Remember: You possess special qualities that only you have. You are a unique individual with a lot to offer. Beauty, confidence and the willingness to accept what life throws your way always comes from within. These are the indicators of strength and self-esteem. We can only change if we want to. Enjoy the person you have become and learn to appreciate the good qualities of others. Look for the positive in everyone and begin to see beauty everywhere you go.

Men do in fact have many wonderful qualities that we need to see. We need to understand that not all men want to hurt us and that not all men have the potential to hurt, abuse or mistreat women. We have to except that men do have loving, caring and tender relationships with their children, spouse, and other women in their lives. We have to learn to trust the men in our lives and give them a chance to be themselves- as men.

*G*etting To Know Yourself In A Sensual Way

The pleasures of the body can only be felt when you allow yourself to let go of all the fears that you possess.

~*Heather Mesaric*

In this unit I will be suggesting that you begin to relate to yourself in a sensual way. This was a challenge for me because I did not feel right touching my body in any way except for basic care. I had to break down the barriers I had built up in my mind to stop limiting my capacity to enjoy normal feelings of sensuality. This section shows you how to venture into the world of pleasure and away from the world of numbness.

I usually experienced a feeling similar to paralysis where I could not feel any sensations on my body when my husband laid his hands on me. Other times, his loving touches and warm hugs made my skin crawl. I would panic and feel a great need to force him away from me. During love making, I had no physical reactions to his caress. When I considered exploring the idea of teaching myself to appreciate sensual touch the concept seemed weird and somewhat revolting.

Children discover their bodies and personal pleasuring at very young ages. Left to their own devices many develop a healthy body appreciation for what feels good and they learn about sensuality by "playing with themselves." This is how they find out that their bodies are beautiful and fun and unless they are told otherwise, they act without guilt or an impression that what they are doing is wrong.

My children would joyfully rub the soap on themselves and giggle. They liked the ticklish feeling while in the bathtub and I would sometimes find them touching themselves in their sleep. It frightened me because I did not know whether or not this behaviour was normal, so I decided to study the subject of masturbation. Reading parenting magazines and books, I found that it was indeed typical and actually necessary for healthy child development. Other parents agreed that it was just another natural milestone that children reached growing up. What an eye opener for me! Still, I could not get past the feeling that touching oneself was dirty and very wrong.

I decided to try to learn more about the gratifying feeling that my children seemed to be experiencing. Bracing myself for yet another new lesson, I was surprised to find a completely different world of enjoyment and I also learned that I could control my body's excitement. I gradually let go of my misunderstandings about sex and sexual satisfaction.

For the first time in my life I was able to please myself and to choose when and how my partner could please me. I decided what I would or could tolerate and what actually felt good for me. My husband became a willing companion as I guided his action for my own sexual arousal and eventual release. It was amazing to be a full participant in a mutually rewarding sexual experience with someone I loved.

Your entire body is sensual/sexual and there are many ways to stimulate your senses. Do not rush the exercises and approach them when you are comfortable doing so. The purpose is to help your body respond to a gentle touch. As you complete various experiments, praise yourself for overcoming any fears that have prevented you from thoroughly enjoying your beautiful body.

As you work through the exercises, you may be aware of some mixed feelings emerging. If memories lead you back to painful reminders of abuse, *stop the exercise*. Give yourself some time to resolve the feelings and then start over again from the beginning of the unit. It is important that you feel in control and comfortable with every step you take. When you have accomplished these assignments on your own, you may choose to have your partner participate with you. If you do, be sure you feel safe and relaxed.

Remember to stop any or all of these exercises at any point, if you feel frightened, sad or angry. You are creating a positive new experience for yourself and you do not want to connect with any past negativity. Don't worry if you feel you need to discontinue the activities a number of times. Be patient and understanding and go at your own pace.

If you need to pause in the steps, it may be very helpful to write in your journal. Detail what you are feeling and look at how you can conquer these emotions. When you have worked through your defences, try the exercise again. It is very important that you do not rush yourself. Remember there are reasons why we feel the way we do about our bodies. You may need a little more time and patience to release the fears or self judgements you are having. Again, I stress, go at your own pace.

You will need to do each exercise on a different day. Do not try to complete more than one at a time. It is really important that you take this process *slowly*.

J*ournal Assignment:* You will require complete privacy and at least half an hour for this exercise. Do this on a daily basis for as long as you need to, in order to get in touch with your normal body sensations. In other words you are finding new ways to <u>re-awaken</u> your <u>dead zones</u>. This is how you will recapture what was lost during sexual abuse. You may find a relaxation exercise from the unit "Releasing Stress And Relaxing," is helpful in preparation.

Remove all of your clothing and either sit in a warm bath or lie on your bed. With the tips of your fingers, gently caress your forehead. Keep stroking your forehead lightly until your fingers create a tingling feeling. Feel the softness of your fingertips. Enjoy the feeling of moving them around your eyes, cheeks, chin and mouth. Continue stroking your face until it has all become alive with tingling sensations. Notice your mouth relaxes into a smile. Do not move on until you can feel the tingling all over your face. It may take a few days to accomplish this in the time allotted and just let yourself be comfortable with whatever you need.

Write in your journal the feelings that emerged while doing this exercise. What did you discover, what did you like or not like about doing this exercise? How did you feel while doing this exercise? Were you relaxed or tense and did you enjoy it?

Do not try the next exercise until you have mastered this one.

*J*ournal Assignment—*Exercise Two:* Allow a little extra time to complete this exercise. Forty-five minutes may be sufficient. Start in the same way as in the exercise above. When you have created the tingling sensation on your face continue to stroke and caress the upper part of your body (avoiding the breasts). Move your fingers over your neck area, shoulders, chest, arms and stomach. Give yourself time to really feel the light touch of your fingers. Take note of which body parts respond warmly to your touch and also, if any seem more sensitive than others. When you have ignited a tingling sensation in these areas, move your fingers down to your lower body (avoiding your genital area). Caress your hips, thighs, legs, and feet. Go slowly and be deliberate with your touch.

Write in your journal how this felt compared to the first time you tried the exercise. Are you beginning to feel different, and if so, how? What do you enjoy about touching your body and what, if anything, bothers you about this process? What do you think when you touch your body in this way?

Do not go on to the next exercise until you have mastered this one. You want to have achieved the same tingling sensation as you did on your face.

*J*ournal Assignment—*Exercise Three:* Start in the same way as in the exercise above. When you have created the tingling sensation on your face, continue to stroke and caress the rest of your body (avoiding your breasts and genitals). Continue with the light touch until you can feel your body reacting warmly. Experiment with both very soft touches and a little firmness using the palms of your hands and at varying speeds. Sample different ways of touching and stroking your body everywhere, again avoid your breasts and genitals. **Do not rush this process.** It is important for you to learn what sensations are pleasurable and which ones feel awkward or uncomfortable. If you feel any nervousness, give yourself permission to feel good about your body and your ability to bring pleasure to it. Feel yourself gently awakening any dead zones that were numbed long ago.

Write in your journal how you felt touching your body. What felt good? Was there a sensation that was different? How was it different? Were there any touches that brought about the desire to touch your breasts and genitals? What were your thoughts while you were touching yourself?

Do not try the next exercise until you have mastered this one.

Journal Assignment—Exercise Four: Start in the same way as in the exercise above. When you have succeeded in creating the tingling sensation on your face move on to caress the rest of your body avoiding your breasts and genitals until you can feel your body reacting to the touch. When your awareness is heightened, gently begin to touch your breasts only. (Do not touch your genitals during this exercise.) Focus on creating a tingling sensation on the nipples and spreading out over the entire breasts. Again, experiment with different pressures and movements as you lovingly stroke your breasts.

Write in your journal your feelings about touching your breasts. What did you like or not like? Were you able to get your breasts to react to different touches?

Do not try the next exercise until you have mastered this one.

Journal Assignment—Exercise Five: Start in the same way as in the previous exercise. When you have created the tingling sensation on your face, body and breasts you should be feeling very relaxed and comfortable. Now, breathe deeply and gently begin to touch your genital area. Do this slowly and notice how it feels. Are you excited? Are you comfortable? Do you have any negative feelings? Learn what feels good and become familiar with the texture, temperature and moisture of your genitals. Let yourself enjoy any feelings of arousal. Use varying strokes and pressures, moving slow, fast or a combination of both. Relax and allow yourself the freedom to bring yourself to a climax, releasing the sexual tension that may surface.

Please note that this cannot happen unless you are comfortable with touching your body. Don't worry if you need to stop and restart the exercise several times to achieve completion. Following your body rhythm is important to becoming stronger and more assured of your ability to experience pleasure by yourself or with someone else. If you would like more information there are a number of books on the market that explain in detail how to master these techniques. One best seller is called "The Big O" by well known female author, Lou Paget.

Journal Assignment—Exercise Six: Write in your journal your feelings about "letting go". Were you afraid of the process? Were you able to get past the awkwardness that you might have felt prior to this experience? Does anything stop you from enjoying the pleasures of your body? If you have experienced your first orgasm, what were your thoughts? Did it surprise you? What are your feelings about being aroused in this manner? Write down what makes you comfortable and what does not. Get in touch with any resolved or continuing misunderstandings of your sensual self. What are your fears and most of all the pleasures of being sexually alive?

Your Week's Affirmations: These are the ones that I used and found very helpful. For the next week say the following affirmations as often as possible in order to create new patterns of "positive thinking." Some days I repeated them more than ten times in an hour or whenever I thought about them. My index cards really helped me to keep saying them often. Remember, you can create your own if these do not say what is in your heart.

Day one: I trust myself; I believe I am beautiful.
Day two: I allow myself to touch my body without fear.
Day three: I am able to enjoy the sensations I am feeling.
Day four: I feel good when I touch myself in certain ways.
Day five: I enjoy the pleasures of my sensual touches.

Day six: I enjoy being gentle and loving with my body.
Day seven: It is okay for me to enjoy my body sexually.

Remember: The exercises in this unit may have been challenging. Congratulate yourself if you faced your fears and did them. The most important lesson that you have learned from these exercises is that you have discovered you can trust yourself. You have complete control over how your body reacts to touch. What a wonderful feeling it must be for you. I know when I overcame this obstacle I felt so different about who I was and what I could do with my life. I felt so free and sensual for the first time. I truly hope you are able to find a way to release the hidden treasures of the body. Give yourself a big hug and buy yourself something special to celebrate the freedom you have just achieved.

*I*ntimacy *In Your Primary Relationship*

In order to fully give of yourself, you must be willing to shed all the masks that you wear so, that your true self becomes one with the other person.

~*Heather Mesaric*

In spite of learning to trust myself and others, understand my needs and enjoy my body I was still not quite sure I could accept my second husband as a true partner in my life. It was a challenge to not become fearful, question his motives and accuse him unfairly.

On some level, I believed he was responsible for my abuse because he was a man. I wanted him, and all men, to hurt the way that I had hurt. He was my unfortunate target in my need to get even with my male abusers. In some ways, I was also testing him to see if he really loved me and would stay in our relationship as he had said he would. I believed that if he left I could say, "I knew he didn't really love me." My sense of being unworthy of his or anyone else's love prompted me to look for faults in order to prove I was a "bad" person deserving of unhappiness.

While I was able to speak about my abuse openly with him, I also kept him at a distance. I gave the impression that I was fragile and expected him to know instinctively what I needed. I used my abuse as an excuse to push him away and then became hurt and angry if he came too close or withdrew. He couldn't win.

With a lot of courage and determination, my husband and I slowly dismantled the defensive walls I'd built. It was frustrating to work through and we finally learned the meaning and experienced the feeling of true intimacy. We spent many days discussing and sometimes just venting our feelings in an effort to dissolve the barriers between us. Finding a workable solution has been the result of our focused energies.

One of the benefits was that I discovered the more I opened up to him, the closer we became. Bringing him into my world of confusion gave me someone to trust and share my journey with. I was rewarded with a loving partner who brought joy and comfort along with his many other special qualities. I began to forgive him for being a "man" and no longer punished him for the sins of others. With his support, I could let go of the past because I knew he believed in me and in our relationship. He was willing to go the distance with me no matter how challenging the journey. We have learned to depend on each other and yet, we remain individuals in our own right.

To move forward I needed to rid myself of some negative thoughts about the man I cared for and loved. I said the following affirmations for a week before I was able to see him in a totally different light. They helped me eliminate my misconceptions of men and allowed my animosity to fade away.

Your *Week's Affirmations:* These are the ones that I used and found very helpful. For the next week say the following affirmations as often as possible in order to create new patterns of "positive thinking." Some days I repeated them more than ten times in an hour or whenever I thought about them. My index cards really helped me to keep saying them often. Remember, you can create your own if these do not say what is in your heart.

Day one: I am able to trust my partner.
Day two: I allow myself to help my partner understand me.
Day three: I love being around my partner, he understands and accepts me.
Day four: I think only loving thoughts about my partner.
Day five: I love my partner for all of his wonderful qualities.

Day six: I accept my partner for who he is.
Day seven: I love being cherished by my partner.

To me, intimacy means allowing someone the privilege of getting to know you at your deepest level. It means peeling off all the outer layers that protect us from getting hurt, feeling vulnerable, scared and lonely. Intimacy includes sharing our dreams and goals. It's a way to let someone else discover the true you. We all have idiosyncrasies that we like about ourselves. Usually, there are also characteristics that make us want to run and hide. We fear revealing them because we believe we risk losing our partner who may judge us. Having a meaningful, intimate relationship means accepting the other person as they are without wanting to make changes.

The intimacy that I am referring to means becoming emotionally naked, letting down our guard and stripping away the facade we usually show the world. This opening-up puts us in a state where we share our greatest fears and triumphs. We break down the barriers that keep us distant not only from ourselves but from others. This level of acceptance offers us a wider knowledge of who we are as individuals and creates the possibility of full acceptance from others.

To have real intimacy you must be able to share and accept your positive and negative feelings about yourself and others. This lets you honestly tell another person what you need and to make better choices for yourself. This familiarity is developed over time and may not always be possible with everyone you want to partner with. Obviously it re-quires a commitment from both parties and an atmosphere of security and respect. Two-way communication is vital to encouraging support and allowing personal growth to be foremost in the relationship.

Intimacy cannot be rushed or demanded. It is earned through openness and understanding. Caring about ourselves and the well-be-ing of the other person is essential to achieving intimacy. You want to support this person in their freedom of expression and recovery from mistakes. Sharing your feelings helps them understand you better and so they feel secure and loved. When you love someone you want to make a difference in their world and create an atmosphere that is unobstructed and honest.

The road to intimacy starts with knowing and believing in yourself. Then you can look in the mirror and say, "I am glad to be me and I am glad you are you."

J*ournal Assignment:* Write in your journal the things that you have not told your partner and give your reasons for not sharing this with them. What stops you from getting close to your partner? List your reasons for keeping your distance or your secrets. The biggest question you need to ask is do you feel safe with this person and if so, why? If not, why not? Also, if you don't feel safe, why are you still there? You need to look at why you feel you can't reveal yourself to the person you are partnered with. Is it embarrassment or a fear that they will not understand or even like you afterwards? You need to examine your reasons for keeping those doors locked. Look at your feelings about sharing things and write down your reasons for not allowing yourself the pleasure of true intimacy with someone. Be honest with your answers. If you can, share this journal writing with your partner so that new beginnings can start to grow between you.

Y*our Week's Affirmations:* These are the ones that I used and found very helpful. For the next week say the following affirmations as often as possible in order to create new patterns of "positive thinking." Some days I repeated them more than ten times in an hour or whenever I thought about them. My index cards really helped me to keep saying them often. Remember, you can create your own if these do not say what is in your heart.

Day one: I like being me, I like who I am.
Day two: I have loving things to say about my partner and myself.
Day three: I like sharing my feelings with my partner.
Day four: I love to discover intimacy with my partner.
Day five: It is okay to share my true feelings.
Day six: I love the choices I make for myself.
Day seven: I love who I am. I love who I am.

Remember: Take the journey of intimacy slowly and don't expect it to develop overnight. This process takes time and you must be willing to share parts of you that you have never shared with anyone before. You need to understand who you are. You must be able to accept, love and cherish the person you are before you can share these qualities with someone else.

Saying The Words "I Love You"

Words are just words, until you mean them.

~*Heather Mesaric*

During my healing process I realized that I was really trying to help myself understand the meaning of unconditional love and why I had never received it. In addition, I wanted to demonstrate this unreserved love towards my children. I knew unconditional love existed because I saw my friends giving love freely and fully to their children and spouses.

Throughout my life, the words "I love you" were always paired with a sexual gesture or the giving of material items for sexual favours. Sometimes I'd hear them when someone wasn't mad or annoyed with me but I had come to believe that saying "I love you" ultimately would involve the act of sex.

I struggled with the knowledge that the way I was shown love was not right. I knew I had no real reference point to use with my own children. It often occurred to me that I was trying to reassure my children by telling them I loved and cared for them, but I was not sure I knew what that entailed.

By loving them as best I could, I discovered that I was learning to love and nurture my own inner child. At times this was challenging because I acted like a child while at the same time trying to be the adult. I was making an effort to heal and accept my inner needs as I used love and understanding to help my own children grow and develop their identities.

The words "I love you" seemed to haunt me and bring emotions that were scary. I was so bewildered by these words that I had a hard time hearing them. My partner would say, "I love you" and I'd think "Yeah, sure." I reminded myself all the time that this reaction was rooted in the past and I gently worked towards believing his words as he meant them to be heard. I pushed through the painful feelings that were evoked and he helped me see that love can be given without strings or conditions attached. He taught me that when someone truly loves you it does not include crossing boundaries. I now know that love is shown through respect and caring for another person's well-being, and taking other people's feelings into consideration. True love creates a safe relationship.

Journal Assignment: Write in your journal your feelings about the words "I love you." Are you able to hear and use them? If so, state what you think is important about these words. If they bring up negative feelings, explain why? What stops you from giving and receiving love from others using these words?

Your Week's Affirmations: These are the ones that I used and found very helpful. For the next week say the following affirmations as often as possible in order to create new patterns of "positive thinking." Some days I repeated them more than ten times in an hour or whenever I thought about them. My index cards really helped me to keep saying them often. Remember, you can create your own if these do not say what is in your heart.

Day one: I deserve to be **loved unconditionally.**
Day two: I am lovable, I am lovable, I am lovable.
Day three: I love you, I love you. It's okay to say I love you.
Day four: I enjoy saying I love you.
Day five: Saying I love you brings me joy and happiness.
Day six: I accept my partner's love and give love in return.
Day seven: I allow love to come into my life.

Remember: Love makes things better. Loving someone and being loved unconditionally by someone is a rewarding feeling that everyone in the world should experience. We all need to be loved and to know that we are lovable. Be less critical and more tolerant of your perceived shortcomings. I believe that we are all special and our "faults" are part of what makes us human. Learn to "lighten-up" with your demands on yourself. Give yourself unconditional love each and every day.

Looking Out The Window

When you are looking out the window,
Your thoughts can scatter to and fro.

When life always seems to be push—pull,
You can become more peaceful.

You can start to dream and admire the beauty,
Especially when you are blue or moody.

You can chase the negative feelings away,
By being more positive throughout the day.

It is the time to welcome the new,
Because your future lies ahead of you.

Believe me it is not that far away,
It comes here day by day.

This allows you time to make a plan,
That you can follow within your life span.

When you are looking out the window,
Life can become as bright as a rainbow.

Look out that window as often as you can,
It brings you closer to your dreams.
As well, it brings you closer to who you want to be,
For today, tomorrow and forever.

—Heather Mesaric

$\mathcal{H}$ealing Through Positive Thinking

Thoughts have a profound way of becoming a reality. Every thought is like a seed, once planted it grows. Be careful what you plant in your mind, you might be planting weeds.

~Heather Mesaric

Most of us spend a lot of time sabotaging our own efforts. We think things will go wrong, that no one cares about us or that our work is never satisfactory. For the longest time I believed deep in my heart that I was unworthy. I thought anything that didn't turn out right was my fault. The little voice inside my head kept saying, "You're not good enough."

I knew I needed to change this way of thinking because I'd gained so much ground in my healing process. I'd spent a great deal of time feeling my feelings and changing the way I thought about myself and the world around me. Even though I had used the daily affirmations and wrote in my journal I wanted to do more. It felt important that I acknowledge all the positive and wonderful things I did and said as I saw my unique self emerging. You too, need to recognize your special gifts and give yourself credit for the incredible person you are.

I believe our well-being depends a lot on how we think and feel about ourselves. It is time to nurture and heal yourself at a deeper level. You need to start acknowledging every positive thought, word and action.

***J**ournal Assignment:* For the next week, write in your journal each day at least 10 things you are proud of yourself for doing. List things you said to people, your accomplishments, work or chores completed and especially self-nurturing and healthy choices. These can be little steps or giant leaps that you took in order to feel good about yourself. Do not forget to mention that you completed this exercise in the first place. You can acknowledge things like getting up on time, doing the laundry, writing the report for work, spending time with your friends or family, completing an exercise from this book and so on. In other words, don't limit your thinking. Be creative and learn to approve of yourself and give yourself credit.

***J**ournal Assignment*—**Exercise Two:** Write at least 10 times each day: "It's great to be me." Every day for the next two weeks, look in the mirror and say, "It's Great To Be Me." Do this often because each time you make this statement to yourself you are strengthening your self-esteem. Saying it out loud gives it even more credibility.

***Y**our Week's Affirmations:* These are the ones that I used and found very helpful. For the next week say the following affirmations as often as possible in order to create new patterns of "positive thinking." Some days I repeated them more than ten times in an hour or whenever I thought about them. My index cards really helped me to keep saying them often. Remember, you can create your own if these do not say what is in your heart.

Day one: I write only positive statements about myself.
Day two: I am very special, I am very special.
Day three: I love being special.
Day four: My thoughts are of kindness, caring and love.
Day five: I completely love myself every day, in every way.
Day six: I love my tender and loving thoughts about myself.
Day seven: I love the way I feel about myself.

Remember: Everything you do is important and is a choice you make. There is beauty in every action we take; so, be proud of what you have to offer yourself and those around you. You are unique; there is no one else like you. Cherish this knowledge. Start thinking positive thoughts about yourself all the time. Believe in your strengths and know that your survival instincts reveal determination and outstanding coping skills. You can and should feel very proud of who you are today.

Your Inner Child

I believe we all have an inner child that has never grown up. Deep inside is the child we were born as—perfect in every way. This child sees the world as a wonderful place to explore with curiosity and spontaneity. In our child we find innocent love and a trust that the world is safe and awesome.

Losing our childhood does not mean our inner child is gone, just disconnected. We still need love and approval and the freedom to discover the world. Now more than ever we need to love and nurture the small person we still harbour within.

My inner child lets me know she is there when I am playing with my own children and feeling joyful. If I am giggling or acting childlike I know I'm expressing emotions from deep within. My self assurances and the kind messages I funnel into my internal dialogue help my inner child feel loved and wanted. At times, I picture myself as a young girl, I say, "I love you" and give myself a hug.

Sometimes my inner child would surface when I remembered something negative from my past. I would get a little sad or annoyed as I realized how much I had missed during my childhood. For me, this was a big obstacle to overcome. For example, in my youth, all our money went to liquor or racetrack gambling so I missed a lot of normal childhood experiences because we "couldn't afford it." Our food, clothing, toys, and Christmas gifts usually came from local churches and charities. To this day, I give to these organizations to help other children and families who do not have the means to survive without assistance. If it hadn't been for the generosity of these groups I would have had nothing. I am very thankful to those who gave with open hearts and kindness. It gives me great pleasure to know that I can help to make a difference in someone else's life.

Journal Assignment: Write in your journal what you would have liked to have done or had as a child that you were not able to. It might have been going to a place you dreamed of, having a new bicycle, learning to swim or skate, getting a special toy or attending birthday parties. You need to be honest with what you wanted and did not get. Describe the feelings you remember about having to miss out.

*Journal Assignment—*Exercise Two: Once you have made your list write down which of these things you can give yourself now. Look at everything and really consider how you can have what you always wanted. You can have a new bike or take those swimming lessons. You can buy yourself that stuffed toy for your bed or even give yourself that long overdue birthday party. You can do ANYTHING you want in order to reclaim your childhood and fulfill the longing inside. Your choices are unlimited.

Your Week's Affirmations: These are the ones that I used and found very helpful. For the next week say the following affirmations as often as possible in order to create new patterns of "positive thinking." Some days I repeated them more than ten times in an hour or whenever I thought about them. My index cards really helped me to keep saying them often. Remember, you can create your own if these do not say what is in your heart.

Day one: The child inside me still lives and needs love.
Day two: I allow my inner child to thrive in me.
Day three: I continue to give myself what I wanted as a child.
Day four: I enjoy nurturing and loving my inner child each day.
Day five: I look at myself through loving and caring eyes.
Day six: I have so much love to give, it is endless.
Day seven: I love, cherish, and respect myself daily.

Remember: If it was love you were lacking, you can give yourself all you need right now. Remember, that while you have been reading and completing the exercises throughout this book, you have been learning to love and approve of yourself. This acceptance is what you need to heal. Love conquers all and is the opposite of hate. It builds while hate destroys. Look at life with loving eyes and express your loving thoughts often. Reach out and give yourself all the love you can as often as you can. Your inner child deserves to be loved. Acknowledge and give a hug to yourself and especially your inner child each and every day.

P*leasing Yourself Instead Of Others*

Putting your own needs ahead of others once in awhile has its rewards.

~*Heather Mesaric*

Before I began healing I was constantly trying to gain people's approval by being available to them, no matter what the cost was to my family and I. When I started to review these behaviours I realized it came from my feelings of unworthiness. I believed that by taking care of others I could camouflage my insecurities and be likable. Continuing to please others was my way of hoping for acceptance, respect and love. I didn't want to see that, in fact, I was being taken advantage of. People constantly used, abused and mistreated me because I was so willing to take anything they dished out in order to feel needed. At times, I wondered why I never got any appreciation and always felt manipulated.

I put all my energies into pleasing others and didn't believe I deserved to be valued or to have anything good in my life. To me, wanting anything in return was equated with being selfish. I presumed that I had to please others in order to feel good about myself.

I constantly put other people's needs ahead of mine and kept busy for all the wrong reasons. I was so desperate for acceptance that I spent all of my waking moments being of service to others. It left me little time to think, eat, and sometimes even sleep. My friends and family called on me day or night. My obsession to be needed led me to choose jobs that required my services on a 24-hour basis. I told myself I must be a great person if everyone needs me. Whenever I found myself suddenly alone or with nothing pressing, I had no idea what to do. Although I spent a lot of time complaining that I never had enough time, in reality, I feared being alone more than anything else.

When I finally took a good look at my life I realized how co-dependent I was. It took many tears and painful struggles to accept that I am lovable and special just as I am. I learned that I did not need to put other people's wishes first in order to feel good about myself. It became easier to say, "No" or "I cannot do that at this time; you will have to find someone else." At first, when I said these words I felt extremely guilty and believed I was letting them down. I reminded myself often that I needed to let go of the guilt and that I too was deserving of my own time and energy. Now, I can say no, or ask myself "Do I really want or need to do this?" I have learned to consider my needs first and everyone else comes second. Also, I have learned that unless you take care of yourself first you really cannot be helpful to others.

Journal Assignment: Make five columns in your journal under the following headings:

Things I Do For Myself Or Others				
Date	For Myself	For Others	Time Spent	My Feelings

For the next week write down all the things you do, record the time you spend on the activity, and what your feelings are about doing it. Be honest. Note whether or not you are feeling guilty, angry, happy, etc. At the end of the week, look over your list and decide if you want to make changes in the way you prioritize yourself and others.

Journal Assignment—**Exercise Two:** Write in your journal your feelings when someone puts other people's needs before yours. Now, write about the tasks that you do for others? How many things do you take on at once? Note how you feel about completing each task. Are you tired or angry with them or yourself? Do you resent helping others? How do you feel when you are not shown sincere appreciation? How do you really feel about giving up your time for others? Be honest; write down your innermost feelings.

Journal Assignment—**Exercise Three:** Look at your list and decide what you would like to let go. Analyze each task to see if you can get someone else involved so you are not doing as much. Do you really need to please others in this way to get their approval, attention, or support? The real question is "Do you need to do this in the first place?" Why can't you say "no," "not this time," or even "I can't do anything for you right now?" It can be a very liberating experience to occasionally say no. Try to expose your underlying reasons for trying to please so much. We always do things for one reason or another—what is your reason for doing what you do?

Journal Assignment—**Exercise Four:** If you cannot say **"no"** then you must do some more work in your journal. Write down the reasons why it is hard for you to say no. Make a list of the feelings that crop up when you even think about saying "no." You must start saying no for your emotional health and to realize that even <u>you</u> cannot please everyone all the time without sacrificing something of yourself. You deserve to be first. Say this for a few days, "I deserve to be first, my needs come first."

Journal Assignment—**Exercise Five:** Write down the number of times you said "no" during the past few days. Has the number changed from previous occasions? Become aware of how often you say yes as opposed to no. Write in your journal *"I can say no for the right reasons. It's okay to say no."* You do not have to say yes in order to please others – only if it pleases you. If you can do what is asked of you and you want to, then do it. Make sure it is because you want to and not because you have to or feel guilty if you don't.

Your Week's Affirmations: These are the ones that I used and found very helpful. For the next week say the following affirmations as often as possible in order to create new patterns of "positive thinking." Some days I repeated them more than ten times in an hour or whenever I thought about them. My index cards really helped me to keep saying them often. Remember, you can create your own if these do not say what is in your heart.

Day one: I feel great about putting my needs first.
Day two: My needs are just as important as other peoples.
Day three: I am able to take care of my needs and desires without guilt.
Day four: I am worthy; I deserve to be taken care of.
Day five: It is great to love myself, all the time.
Day six: I love putting my needs first.
Day seven: I deserve to have my needs met.

I now do the things I want to do without the guilt or burden of taking on too much. I'm able to evaluate whether I want or need to do what others ask of me and what I might have to forfeit in the process. I believe that I come first and can put my husband and children's needs ahead of mine if I choose to. The power to say yes or no lies within me. I can do what I want, when I want and how I want. I believe my needs are more important than anything else in my life.

Remember: You have the ability to decide whether you want to do something for someone or not. Do not feel guilty if you choose to say "no." You deserve to be happy and you deserve to come first. If you take care of your needs then you will be much better able to be available for others. You must remember you always have a choice.

CONGRATULATIONS

Be Proud of your accomplishment to date. You have won first prize for completing your own personal marathon. Pat yourself on the back and relish your victory. You are special and now you can celebrate the new life you create for yourself each and every day.

Write these words on paper and put them up on your bedroom wall.

"I am a Special Person"

Enlightenment Healing

*H*ow To Use The
"Enlightenment Healing" Section

This section will deal with topics you can continue to work on for the rest of your life. It is intended to help you establish a positive lifestyle that can easily be maintained.

I have mentioned several times in this book that I feel healing is a lifelong journey. This unit is the beginning of your new way of being and offers you insight into other ways to live a life of promise and positive change. Most of all it gives you ownership of your personal potential and encourages you to keep your mind open to new ideas.

Throughout this book I have offered you guidelines for developing ways to create a safe and supportive environment. In this section I give more suggestions and I challenge you to make changes that will affect you today and in your future.

*L*iving In The Present

The past is gone, tomorrow is not here yet, therefore, I only have today.

~*Heather Mesaric*

The concept of living for today is hard for most of us to handle. We have a tendency to live in the past or at least allow the past to heavily influence how we live now. We plan and dream about what tomorrow will bring, based on the way the past has unfolded. It affects our every move, the decisions we make and our interactions with the world around us.

However, this way of thinking, really gives away our ability to live today and robs us of the pleasures that living in the moment offers. We miss out on precious time because we are distracted by what "has been" or what "might be."

To a certain extent memories are important in helping us know who we are and what experiences have helped shape our lives. Planning for the future gives us a reason to set goals and have hope for the things we dream of. We need both of these dimensions to have a balanced life. As we've seen through this process it is not healthy to live only in the past, nor is it good to spend a lot of our time wishing and waiting for tomorrow to come.

If we live for today, then we can acknowledge the past and put it where it belongs, behind us. It is over and we move on because we know it has no power over us. We have learned how to take control of our lives and choose to recall memories that give us positive or warm feelings. This is what empowers us and guides us into a happier future.

If we live in the "today," the future can also be put in its proper place. We can do things that will affect how tomorrow turns out such as paying our bills, saving for retirement or vacations. Being in the "here and now" makes us aware of what we need to do today so that the future is more comfortable physically and emotionally.

What we must not do is spend all our time dreaming of how things could be by constantly thinking "if only we did this or that." We must make sure that we are realistic in our goals and understand that sometimes things don't happen just the way we planned. Remember we have no control over how tomorrow will evolve.

Living in the "here and now" means just that, enjoy the moment for what it is. Life in the "today" has so much to offer and it's there for you to experience and cherish. You can feel so much more pleasure and enjoy life to its fullest if you live every minute in the "here and now". Yesterday is gone and tomorrow has not arrived. The only day you can really participate in is today. None of us knows how many "tomorrows" we will have. Take each day as it comes and live it to the fullest. Don't waste today dreaming of the future or crying over the past.

As I healed my wounds, I told myself that staying in the here and now gave me the power to make of my life exactly what I wanted. This helped me to make plans for the days ahead and reflect on all the positive changes I'd made to date. I was able to treasure everything that came my way and eliminate unnecessary worries and uncertainties.

In the past, I struggled for control and I always felt something was missing when my life was not going the way I wanted it to. This began to change when I started living in the "here and now." I learned to take each and every day for what it was. Sometimes it was a day to relax and enjoy some free time and other days I completed tasks. I even gave myself some time to dream about my future without becoming too separate from "today." I always made sure I did something or said something to myself and to someone else that brought me joy and pleasure. Now, I really see every day as being special and I find ways to make the world a better place.

Journal Assignment: Write in your journal your habits surrounding living in the past or future. Do you spend time wishing things could be different and wondering why some things happened the way they did? Do you find yourself thinking "If only ..." or do you live in the future dreaming of what might be? Where do your thoughts go on a daily basis? Get in touch with where you are spending your days and note any patterns you discover. Keep a diary of your thoughts and feelings and then jot in the symbols ***"P"*** for the past, ***"F"*** the future or ***"T"*** for today. Count the "P's, F's, and T's" to see where you send your mind throughout your waking hours. Be vigilant to make sure you pay attention to every theme going through your mind.

With this knowledge, you can change the balance in your thoughts. You are trying to have more "T's (today) and fewer "F's (future) and "P's (past). Remember it's okay to have the past and future in your thoughts if they have a positive effect on your "today."

Your Week's Affirmations: These are the ones that I used and found very helpful. For the next week say the following affirmations as often as possible in order to create new patterns of "positive thinking." Some days I repeated them more than ten times in an hour or whenever I thought about them. My index cards really helped me to keep saying them often. Remember, you can create your own if these do not say what is in your heart.

Day one: Living in the "here and now" is possible for me.
Day two: Today, I see all the beauty life has to offer me.
Day three: I have peace of mind, in the present.
Day four: Living in the present allows me to have control.
Day five: Today, I love myself to the fullest.
Day six: Today, I have control over my life.
Day seven: Today, I will trust and love myself.

Remember: Relax and take pride in your new way of living. You have so much to rejoice over, while living in the present. This does not mean you won't face disappointments or sad times. It means you keep your focus on the present and see events around you in a different light. It is often said, "This too shall pass" and you have the power to wade through any difficulty if you stay in the moment. I truly believe that things we label as "bad" happen for a reason just as much as the things we think are "good." When things go wrong, I try to understand the reason and look for a positive in the negative. It's the "silver lining" we find when we are willing to face life head-on. For example, when my husband lost his job we felt frightened because we had become dependent on his income. With our thoughts focused on the positive he soon found another job that actually paid more money. ***Positive thinking changes everything***.

*B*elieving In Yourself

Believe it can be done. When you believe something can be done, really believe, your mind will find the ways to do it. Believing a solution paves the way to solution.

~David Schwarts

Survivors such as you and I often have to struggle with trying to make people believe us. In my case, I doubted my own capabilities and questioned my motives and thoughts. I had lost my ability to function on my own and had no sense of purpose in my life. The result was that I had great difficulty believing in myself.

I knew that I needed to learn to stop putting myself down for everything that went wrong. I had to learn to trust myself even if I wasn't always sure I deserved it.

It wasn't easy to accept the fact that I did not always know what was right, but I knew I was doing my best at any given moment. If I made a decision that turned out to be "wrong," I trusted that I had done what I could with the information I had at the time.

I had to tell myself often that if I wanted to make changes I needed to live as the person I wanted to be. In other words, I had to believe I could change. I had to know that I could trust in my own power to shift my thoughts and actions.

Remember the childhood story of the little engine struggling up the side of the mountain? As he puffed his heavy load up the hillside he kept repeating *"I think I can, I think I can, I think I can."* When he finally reached the top he shouted "I thought I could, I thought I could, I thought I could." This little book has a strong message not only for children but adults as well. A simple phrase like "I think I can" reminds us that if we put our minds to it, we just might succeed.

The one positive thing my foster father told me was to say to myself every night before I went to sleep "I can do anything I want to, if I put my mind to it." In spite of the adversity, I was able to use this strategy for many things in my life. This included persevering to get my College degree, writing this book, conducting workshops and retreats. Most of all, it helped me to believe I really could do anything I set my mind to.

Believing in oneself brings many rewards that will never be known unless you are willing to take the risk. There is no limit to what you can do if you believe in yourself.

Journal Assignment: Write in your journal at least ten times "I believe I can do anything I want to do." Believe in yourself and keep reinforcing your trust in your capabilities. Looking into a mirror, pat yourself on the back and say, "I am wonderful, there is no one like me. I have the ability to do anything I want to do." Do this several times a day during the week.

Journal Assignment—Exercise Two: Find the story of the little engine either in your home, the library or a bookstore. The title is "The Little Engine That Could" and the author is Watty Piper. Read it over several times. Even if you are familiar with the story re-read it to refresh your memory. Let the meaning of this classic story influence you to be strong and motivated. Think of ways you can adopt these inspirational principles into your daily life.

You must keep focusing on all your positive traits. Remind yourself that you are a very able and loving individual. Stand tall, be proud of who you are and all that you have accomplished.

Your Week's Affirmations: These are the ones that I used and found very helpful. For the next week say the following affirmations as often as possible in order to create new patterns of "positive thinking." Some days I repeated them more than ten times in an hour or whenever I thought about them. My index cards really helped me to keep saying them often. Remember, you can create your own if these do not say what is in your heart.

Day one: I believe I can do anything I want.
Day two: I believe I am wonderful, talented and special.
Day three: I am proud of who I am and what I have done.
Day four: I believe in myself, I believe in myself.
Day five: I love believing in my accomplishments.
Day six: I believe I have so much to offer the world.
Day seven: I always believe in myself and what I do.

Remember: Be proud of how far you have come and celebrate your successes, not your failures. Look at the things that didn't work out as times when you needed to practice a new skill. You did not fail if you tried something and it did not work out. It gives you another opportunity to practice something else that's new and different. Think about how a baby learns to walk. With our positive encouragement they keep trying to make it happen. Think of the new talents you have learned over a lifetime like driving a car, using a computer, preparing meals etc. If you believe in yourself nothing can stop you from doing your best. You have the power to do what ever you want and because you are a survivor you *can do anything.*

$\mathcal{P}$romoting Acceptance

The first step towards change is awareness. The second step is acceptance.

~*Nathaniel Branden*

What does acceptance really mean? It encompasses everything that we have been dealing with throughout this book. Acceptance allows you to take hold of your life and live it freely.

Give yourself a moment to reflect on all the changes that you have gone through since staring this process. See how differently you view yourself and your life today. Notice how wonderful you are feeling and how much pride you have in yourself for the hard work that has brought you this far. These changes have altered your life in a very substantial way. Look in the mirror and smile at the new you with loving and accepting eyes because you know that you are responsible for the progress you have made.

Accepting ourselves for whom we are and what we have to offer can sometimes be a little difficult. My biggest hurdle was allowing myself the chance to heal in the first place. The next thing I needed to do was to set myself free and lower the restrictions I had placed on my personal growth. By looking at your strengths you will find lots to cheer about and know you are well prepared for any tough times you might face.

Enjoy the freedom that you have worked so hard to achieve. Make sure that you do not let yourself or anyone else be a saboteur. Never again belittle yourself or your efforts because the truth is that you really are remarkable.

Accepting who you are means being respectful of yourself at all times. It also means celebrating all your accomplishments; the ones you see through to the end and those that don't ever seem to be complete. Being able to see your mistakes with honest observation takes courage. Don't forget that mistakes are lessons learned for the next time. Be kind and gentle with yourself always. Love yourself for who you are, no matter what.

Journal Assignment: Write in your journal all the achievements you have made throughout this healing process. Point form is all you need. The purpose of this exercise is to make you aware of all the positive changes you have manifested. You will see that you have truly come a long way.

I believe that with all this hard work I have found the real "me." I had been here all along, but well hidden in fear of showing the world who I was. I have taken the time to look inside and no longer have to protect or hide my beautiful self. The answers I was searching for have been uncovered from the secret places within. Listen to yourself and trust that you too will find your way.

Your Week's Affirmations: These are the ones that I used and found very helpful. For the next week say the following affirmations as often as possible in order to create new patterns of "positive thinking." Some days I repeated them more than ten times in an hour or whenever I thought about them. My index cards really helped me to keep saying them often. Remember, you can create your own if these do not say what is in your heart.

Day one: I love who I am, and who I have become.
Day two: I accept myself for who I am.
Day three: I accept myself; I have so much to learn.
Day four: I accept myself. I truly love myself.
Day five: I embrace myself with love and respect.

Day six: I admire and cherish the changes I continue to make.
Day seven: Acceptance means loving myself completely.

Remember: You cannot love anyone else until you fully love yourself. The same goes for acceptance; you must first accept yourself before you can offer the same understanding and respect to others. Acceptance makes room for "human-ness" and forgives missteps. It embraces both mistakes and personal growth so that we learn to love ourselves and each other, no matter what. Don't ever forget that you are extraordinary in your own right. Accept that you are an exquisite human being with so much to share with yourself and others. Give yourself a big hug, look in the mirror and say, "I love you with all my heart."

$\mathcal{R}$ebuilding Your Life

Starting over means you get to tear down the walls that were preventing you from seeing the world in all its splendour.

~*Heather Mesaric*

Moving forward in our lives means making room for new experiences. Think of what would happen if you kept everything you had ever acquired. Eventually you would run out of storage and have to move. The same thing happens with our mind. We need to get rid of the old negative thinking patterns and make room for our new healthy ones.

I believe that by releasing your past you create space in your life for more positive opportunities. You don't have to deny the abuse to let it go. Simply choose to move ahead and construct a life of meaning and fulfillment. Accept all that has taken place within and around you and allow yourself to go forward.

Acceptance and forgiveness are the key elements for healing. Love yourself enough to let go of the past so you can build a new foundation for yourself and your family. You can chart the course of history from this day on and you can help materialize a future rich with endearing memories.

You have been learning how to treat yourself with love and now you must put everything you have learned into practice.

Journal Assignment: Write in your journal these words: "My life is my own. I can make my future what I want it to be." Do this several times over the next few days until you really believe it is within your grasp.

***Journal Assignment—*Exercise Two:** Now write about how you want your future to look. This is the time to dream a little. If you could have anything, do anything, own anything, what would your future look like? Write down how you want your life to be, how you want your family to treat you, the job, the money, the house. Do not hold anything back or get stuck thinking something is unattainable. Just write out your future dream world as you would like it to be. Write as little as you think you need or as much as you want. If you can, write in the present tense as though what you want has actually happened. It's a way of seeing the life you imagine as it looks in the present moment. I call this making a "Dream Life." The following is a short version of some of my entries:

My Life Today

"*I am now a successful author. I have a 5 bedroom house. My home and family life is a close-knit and caring unit. I am very happy, healthy and my life has so much to offer me each and every day. Life is great, I have everything I need, want and desire.*"

***Journal Assignment—*Exercise Three:** Copy your "Dream Life" onto several sheets of paper (I chose to put mine on pages with bright rainbows). Title each page, "MY LIFE TODAY." Frame one copy and place it in a prominent location where you will see it every day and often. Tape up the others all over your home where you will be sure to run into them on a regular basis. Mine appeared in my bedroom by the light switch, on the bathroom cabinet mirror, on the cupboard over the kitchen sink, in the laundry room, along the basement stairs, on the car dashboard, at the front door, etc. Each time you hang a note, read it over (out loud is best) and really absorb the message. Find places you frequent and read the notes every time you pass one. The more you read it the more your subconscious mind will make things happen for you. I wanted to make sure I would see my "Dream Life" every time I moved from room to room in my house. At the time, I really wanted all these things in my life so, I made sure I re-affirmed these statements throughout my day.

*J*ust remember to keep these dreams in the present as much as possible. You are proclaiming that this is your life now. The things that you want will appear in your life very quickly, or you may find situations transpire to help lead you to fulfilling these desires. You might see your dream job advertised or drive by the house you have been longing to buy and noticing it is now for sale. The world will open up for you and you will find people, things and situations coming together to aid in the process. The most important key to making this work is to keep it in the present – believing and proclaiming you already have what you want. Honestly, this works. I've seen it in my own life and the lives of those around me.

*Y*our *Week's Affirmations:* These are the ones that I used and found very helpful. For the next week say the following affirmations as often as possible in order to create new patterns of "positive thinking." Some days I repeated them more than ten times in an hour or whenever I thought about them. My index cards really helped me to keep saying them often. Remember, you can create your own if these do not say what is in your heart.

Day one: My life starts with the positive changes I make today.
Day two: I believe I always make the best choices for myself.
Day three: I continue to make room for new experiences to enter my life.
Day four: Life is full of change. I welcome these changes with an open heart.
Day five: I embrace my new way of living.
Day six: I love to explore new ideas and experiences.
Day seven: Life is wonderful and my life is mine to enjoy.

*R*emember: You have the ability to change your life from now on. If you accept and embrace the person you have become you can cherish your life from this day forward. You are a great person who deserves to have all the treasures that life has to offer: health, happiness, wealth etc. Learn to accept the joy of you.

*M*aking Positive Changes

Those who have found their way, find delight in knowing that they have conquered their worst fears.

~Heather Mesaric

This book has taken you through many stages of my journey of healing from the trauma of physical, emotional, and sexual abuse. I hope it has helped you to find your own way to recovery and that you have also realized support through sharing your story with someone else.

The purpose of the book was to show you that you can change your life. By shifting your thinking about yourself and the world around you, you have empowered yourself to believe you can do anything.

Sometimes we need help from others for that extra push over a forbidding hurdle. Other times you might prefer to work through situations alone. If I catch myself in negative self-talk, I forgive my slip and re-word my inner dialogue. Getting into stressful circumstances can cause self-ridicule and I know I must be gentle with myself if this happens. Remember that perfection is unattainable. When changes do not occur as rapidly as you think or want them to, relax and let it go. Be a friend to yourself and trust that things will turn around in due course.

When you want to alter something about yourself remember to evaluate the reasons it seems important to you. Having a clear picture of why you think you need to modify a behaviour will bring about change more quickly. Try to correct only one thing at a time because shifting habits takes focus and effort. You may get discouraged trying to change too much at once and these feelings can cause you to give up on yourself.

When you have made a significant change in your life be sure to enjoy the new feelings <u>before</u> you work on something else. The benefits are not always immediately visible. Sometimes the value of what you have gained is more obvious to others than even to you.

Set small and achievable goals so you can see yourself progressing. It will also help you to determine which methods work best for you. Being successful will keep you motivated especially when dealing with lifetime addictions such as drinking, smoking, drug use or unhealthy eating patterns.

I strongly recommend that you seek guidance from a trained professional if you are trying to stop an addiction. Find someone with expertise in the area you need so you have a knowledgeable resource to answer questions and provide support.

Anything you do to your body that is harmful, painful or in excess is self-abuse. I believe that you can abuse your body in many ways. This includes the obvious such as over-eating, under-eating, smoking, alcohol consumption, taking drugs (both illegal and by prescription) to lesser known addictions involving excessive exercising, caffeine use, workholism, co-dependency relationships and even indiscriminate sex.

Substance abuse ***numbs*** the body and mind creating an addiction. Any addiction serves a purpose and you need to look at why you gravitate to a substance or behaviour. We sometimes try to fool ourselves by giving excuses for our self-defeating habits. We may say we enjoy coffee because it relaxes us or gets us going in the morning. If we are really honest with ourselves, we will acknowledge that it is a perfect detractor from the pain and this justifies our need to continue. In reality all addictions prevent us from releasing the pain and going forward. Addictions keep us in a victim mode and only really serve to hinder our progress.

***J*ournal Assignment:** Write in your journal what addictions or other forms of self-abuse you engage in. Include the ones that seem "harmless" like coffee and sugar as well as more threatening ones like alcohol and drugs. Please be honest. This is your private list and is the place where you most need to be real with yourself. Beside each entry write your reasons for continuing with this addiction. The length of the list does not matter as much as what you reveal to yourself. You need to understand what your addictions are and what need they fulfill in you.

Journal Assignment—Exercise Two: Write in your book some of the ways that you can begin to change these behaviours. Include things like talking to a friend, getting a smoking patch from the doctor, starting a healthy diet, seeking professional help for alcohol or drug addiction, finding self-help groups which deal with your cravings, etc. Become familiar with the choices that you have to help you break the addictive cycle.

Journal Assignment – Exercise Three: Write in your journal this promise to yourself "I will no longer abuse my body, I love myself too much to destroy my body. I promise I will no longer abuse my body with ….." List each abusive habit you want to change.

If you write down alcohol, drugs or other harmful substance, I stress you should seek professional assistance. Stopping some addictions can have very uncomfortable side effects which can be managed with medical treatment.

I was not able to give up some of my addictions without the help of my doctor. Being pregnant, I knew I had to make changes if I wanted a healthy baby. I chose to eliminate my daily 10 cups of coffee, 4-5 chocolate bars, cigarettes and once-a- week drinking at the bars. My diet was especially critical because I developed gastro diabetes during each of my pregnancies.

My motivation was pregnancy and yours might be self-love or a desire to compliment the new beginnings you have created. Whatever your reasons, be proud of yourself for wanting to make the change. Some changes can happen overnight while others need time to unfold. Be gentle with yourself and listen to your body.

*Y*our Week's Affirmations: These are the ones that I used and found very helpful. For the next week say the following affirmations as often as possible in order to create new patterns of "positive thinking." Some days I repeated them more than ten times in an hour or whenever I thought about them. My index cards really helped me to keep saying them often. Remember, you can create your own if these do not say what is in your heart.

Day one: I support the changes that I am making in my life.
Day two: I am gentle with myself; I accept change in a loving manner.
Day three: I seek the guidance I need for my addictions.
Day four: I welcome the opportunity to make changes.
Day five: I continue to modify my habits in loving ways.
Day six: I allow myself to see the benefits of change.
Day seven: I love the changes I make with my life. I love myself.

*R*emember: Making positive changes can be both rewarding and a little frightening. It is important that you believe in what you are doing and that you set yourself up to succeed. Do not give up hope and continue to do your best. *Changes do take time. Be patient and continue to give yourself the love and understanding that you deserve.*

$\mathcal{E}$nding The Cycle Of Abuse

Standing up for oneself prevents the bully from continuing to threaten and hurt you. Stand up and say "no, not ever again will you harm me or anyone else."

~Heather Mesaric

There was a time when I rarely stood up for myself. I remember situations in which I allowed people to treat me badly and call me names because I didn't believe I was worthy of anything better. For quite some time I honestly thought I had a sign on my forehead reading "Abuse me. I deserve it." I kept attracting people into my life who were cruel and did not care about me. This resulted in my being criticized, belittled and being exposed to other unmentionable attacks.

In order for me to believe that I could end the cycle of abuse I had to overcome many barriers both within myself and those I saw in the world around me. I worked hard to live the principles of self-care in my home. It meant setting boundaries with and for my children so they felt comfortable and safe. They learned to treat themselves with respect and to speak up if they had any questions or concerns. My husband and I committed to never using bad language, drinking to excess or indulging in other self-abusive behaviours that would set a bad example for them. We spoke words of love in our home and showed a willingness to help those less fortunate. We sang songs and played games with our children that offered them a fun, safe and nurturing environment to grow and develop through the normal stages of childhood.

Stopping the cycle of abuse means getting involved. We have to educate our families, our communities, the general population and especially each other. This starts with working in our own homes to create a safe place for everyone. Most importantly, we must ensure that our children have the skills to empower themselves. While we need to set and protect boundaries for ourselves, we also need to teach others to do the same. Open, honest communication will ultimately break the silence and prevent the secrecy that allows abuse to proliferate. We can put an end to abuse.

Journal Assignment: Write in your journal about any situations where you have taken steps to stop the abusive cycle. List times when you have made circumstances safe for yourself and others. If you have children, how is your home a haven for them? If it isn't, why isn't it? It is absolutely critical that you put a halt to any abuse in your home environment. If necessary, move yourself and your children to safety for the well-being of everyone.

Ending the cycle may require courage and determination but the long-term effects of abuse are more difficult to conquer. You can stop abusive situations instantly by making the decision to be proactive and responsible. It begins with you and you can be the catalyst for change.

Your Week's Affirmations: These are the ones that I used and found very helpful. For the next week say the following affirmations as often as possible in order to create new patterns of "positive thinking." Some days I repeated them more than ten times in an hour or whenever I thought about them. My index cards really helped me to keep saying them often. Remember, you can create your own if these do not say what is in your heart.

Day one: I am able to stop the cycle of abuse.
Day two: I am involved in putting a stop to abuse.
Day three: I make healthy choices to stop abuse.

Day four: I do everything I can to make my home safe.
Day five: I listen to my heart. I am safe.
Day six: I love myself; I am able to stop my own cycle of abuse.
Day seven: The cycle of abuse stops with me.

Remember: In order to stop abuse we must believe that we are strong and that we have been successful in rebuilding our lives. We need to know that we no longer have to be afraid or ashamed of what happened to us. While we may be the "result" of abuse, we are not the cause and have healed ourselves from the suffering of its devastating consequences. We have a right to educate others on how to change the public's perception of the effects of abuse. My personal devotion to ending the cycle of abuse has guided me to write this book to encourage others to change the world around them. It really does start with you and me. We must let others know that we will no longer tolerate or be silenced by the abusers in our society. Give yourself a big hug and be proud of your breakthroughs.

I Once Was

A person who never asked questions;
I did not care.
A person who never laughed but;
Always cried.
A person who never knew the meaning of love, joy, faith or inner wisdom;
I was too skeptical.
A person who never saw the beauty that surrounded me;
I was too blind to see.
A person who never heard the children play;
I did not want to hear what I missed.
A person who never saw life as it really could be;
I was in too much pain.
A person who never opened my eyes;
I was too afraid of what I might see.
A person who never spoke about the things that troubled me;
I was afraid I would not be believed or heard.
A person who was always lonely;
Even when others were around.
A person who never knew what love was;
I did not feel I was worth it.
A person who underestimated my abilities to do anything;
I did not feel I was good enough.
A person who did not feel good about myself or the world around me;
I did not think people approved of me.
A person who never looked in the mirror;
I was afraid of what I might discover about the reflection I saw.
I once was a person who never opened my eyes, ears, mouth or heart;
But now, "once" is truly in my past.

—Heather Mesaric

240

*M*aking A Difference

When I reach out to help others, I help to change the world. I help the world become a better place.

~Heather Mesaric

My life ambition has always been to make a difference for those who have experienced abuse of any kind. I have spent many years educating myself and others to make our world a safer place to live.

The boundaries that I have helped my children create have allowed them to feel safe and secure. I have broken the silence by sharing with my children, family, friends and others what took place in my childhood. This has helped them to become more aware of the effects of my abuse and understand the trauma I have lived with most of my life.

My willingness to speak up has also prompted other family members to look at their role in supporting or denying my abuse. This experience has made lasting changes in their lives whether they know it or not. I will never again be hushed for the silence destroys and eventually distorts the facts. Now, I hold my head up high as I speak the truth that so many sexual abuse survivors have concealed from the world.

I believe that because I have allowed myself to heal, my children have the opportunity to grow and understand their world in a different way. I have so much to thank my children for because my healing process really started with their births. They have given me the strength and a reason to go on and to make a difference in not only my life but the lives of many others. I have modeled for them a life of courage and resilience in triumphing over something so potentially disabling.

By taking a stand, I believe we all have the capacity to make a difference. As we grow stronger, we need to help those who cannot help themselves. By loving ourselves we are able to love others. We can and do make a difference.

I believe that if we treated ourselves as we would our children we would create a world of compassion and love. The ripple effect would start with our own inner child and expand to fill the universe with its many millions of people needing to be loved. We all deserve kindness and understanding. Small children who feel safe and nurtured have an amazing ability to be forgiving and they love life. They are the true examples of living in the moment and can teach us so much about enjoying this world. We need to open up our hearts and rekindle the childlike qualities we all possess to fully experience the splendour of our existence.

Journal Assignment: Write in your journal the wonderful attributes of the very young children you know. If you do not have children of your own think of those of friends or relatives or even children in your neighbourhood. Usually children under the age of five still hold the characteristics I am referring to. What behaviours do they exhibit when they are mad, happy, excited, frightened? Who do they go to, how do they try to solve their problems? How do they show that something is bothering them or that they want attention? Write down all these characteristics and if necessary observe them for a few days to be sure you are seeing them under a variety of circumstances.

*B*e aware of the innocence that children have and their ability to forgive and go on with their lives. See if you notice that they interact without any worry, fear or judgments of the people around them.

Journal Assignment—**Exercise Two:** Write in your journal some of the things that you know you can do to make a difference – for yourself and for others. Can you break the silence? Have you revealed your experiences? If so, to whom? List the things that you feel you could do in your home, your family, your community or the world in general. Think about places you could offer support through volunteer time. Read notices in your local paper or contact service agencies to see what is needed. Keep notes on your ideas for helping to prevent abuse.

Your Week's Affirmations: These are the ones that I used and found very helpful. For the next week say the following affirmations as often as possible in order to create new patterns of "positive thinking." Some days I repeated them more than ten times in an hour or whenever I thought about them. My index cards really helped me to keep saying them often. Remember, you can create your own if these do not say what is in your heart.

Day one: I trust myself enough to break my silence.
Day two: I know I can make a difference.
Day three: I am speaking out about my abuse.
Day four: I am able to let others know about my abuse in a positive way.
Day five: I use my voice to be heard. I break my silence about the abuse.
Day six: I break my silence; I am making a difference for others and myself.
Day seven: I love myself; I am able to make a difference with my life.

Remember: You have what it takes to make a difference. Know that you have so much to offer and can help change how the world views sexual abuse. You can be an inspiration to those struggling to find their own voice. Most importantly, you can stop abuse in your home, extended family and community by speaking up and speaking out. I wish you well and I know that together we make a difference. Love yourself enough to say, "I'll do it."

God Is There For Me

In the quietness of my place,
God touches my face.

Through my prayers he speaks to me,
God tells me to let things be.

I share my feelings through and through,
God reassures me I have done all I can do.

God gave me the gift to feel his presence from above,
In return, I give him all my love.

When things get hard for me to continue and I lose hope,
God gives me the strength to find ways in order to cope.

At night when my heart is filled with sadness and tears,
God sends angels to my room to take away all my fears.

When I opened the door to my heart and gave away the key,
God lets me know that he is always there for me.

—Heather Mesaric

*U*nderstanding Your Spirituality

The relationship between man and God is between them and them alone.

~*Heather Mesaric*

My relationship with God has fluctuated throughout my life. There were times when I was angry with him for allowing the abuse to take place and not helping me out of my terrible ordeals. My first child died three hours after birth and at this and many other times, it seemed no one heard my prayers. Yet there were other occasions when I felt His presence and love. I knew God was with me when I did give birth to four beautiful, healthy children. He blessed me with a second (and very loving) marriage and he gave me my life's work. Through him I have found the perfect career as an advisor to children and adults who need someone they can trust with their troubles in daily life. He helped me press ahead with this book and supports me in my workshops, seminars and with other writings. There are many more ways that God has blessed me but most of all it's with the faith to believe and heal myself in order to help others.

My love of God was often denied when I felt bitter, angry, fearful, untrusting and alone. I became closer to God as my healing process mended my wounds and dissipated my resentments towards life.

We are all individuals and our acceptance and understanding of our spirituality is individual. I believe that our spirituality depends on our awareness of who we are and what we want from our lives.

My own search has taken me in many different directions and I know that there is a power greater than me. This higher power has been with me throughout my healing process but also during my entire life. I was just unaware. I don't know that I fully understand the meaning of spirituality but I do know the answers will be revealed to me when I am ready.

Trusting my instincts to make changes in my life has helped me develop a clear understanding of my own sense of spirituality. I know that I will follow the right path for me and that I will never be alone.

My spirituality and healing process are a lifelong journey and are totally connected. I cannot separate or understand one without the other. Nor can I deny the fact that they both exist and have been present within me all my life.

I believe in God, I always have and I always will. Although I didn't always know it, God has been there for me to talk to and has helped me throughout my life. I haven't always felt that he helped me when I needed him most, but I have certainly felt his presence in my darkest hours of healing and during the abuse. It was my belief in God that held me up through some of the most terrifying experiences of my life.

Our desire to strive for the best by helping others and giving to those less fortunate is an indication that we believe in something. It may be God or another higher power or even each other. I believe in being human and that there is a purpose for all of us. I know that if we work at it we can make this world a safer place. We can't be passive and must evaluate what is important to us, go after it and change what needs changing for the betterment of humankind.

I believe that spirituality is oneness, a form of togetherness, with all of us working alone yet with each other. Also, I believe love is the foundation of our spirituality. We cannot be open to a higher power if we do not have love in our hearts. Loving ourselves makes it possible to know the power of the universal love that is greater than anyone on earth can imagine.

J*ournal Assignment:* Write in your journal about your belief system. Do you believe in God or a higher power that you may call by any name? Each religious group has a different name for God; what is yours? Do you believe in him, if so, why? If not, why not? Are you religious? Are you spiritual? What is the difference to you? Begin to explore your feelings about a higher power and get in touch with your own spirituality.

Your Week's Affirmations: These are the ones that I used and found very helpful. For the next week say the following affirmations as often as possible in order to create new patterns of "positive thinking." Some days I repeated them more than ten times in an hour or whenever I thought about them. My index cards really helped me to keep saying them often. Remember, you can create your own if these do not say what is in your heart.

Day one: I believe in the strength that lives within me.
Day two: I trust my needs will be taken care of.
Day three: My spirituality will continue to grow, as I do.
Day four: I am open to learning about my own spirituality.
Day five: I love myself, I love who I am and I feel loved.
Day six: I believe in something greater than myself.
Day seven: I seek the truth. The truth is within me.

Remember: Spirituality comes from within. It offers us many choices and solutions to ongoing questions. In order to benefit from your own spirituality you must be open to receiving its good and willing to acknowledge it exists. Look inside for the answers you need and find your own path to a spiritual connection. When you do, you will feel deep, empowering love for yourself and others. You will begin to understand why you are here and realize that every one of us needs to feel loved.

Lifetime Healing

*M*y Life Has Just Begun

I start my new life today and look forward to the new challenges that life has to offer.

~*Heather Mesaric*

My healing journey has taken me from an individual who was angry, fearful, confused and misguided to someone feeling safe, happy, loved and most of all, thankful for my life. I am passionate about continuing to grow and develop new ideas that nurture my positive feelings towards myself and others. This enables me to maintain a healthy perspective and live my life with the freedom to be me.

The following is my lifetime commitment to myself. In many ways, the long journey I have taken starts now, right here at this precise moment in time.

I have written down promises to myself and posted them in my bedroom as a reminder of how far I have come. It proves my determination and that I am deserving of happiness. I wrote these to support my lifetime healing and to make sure that I am never again abused or allow anyone else to be abused.

I want to stop abuse from happening everywhere in the world and I am dedicated to furthering my support of others. Make your own list of pledges to reflect how you will fulfill the promises you have made to yourself on this journey of healing.

My Promise To Myself

I **promise** to remember I am a survivor – not a victim.
I **promise** to treat myself with kindness and respect.
I **promise** to put myself first before others.
I **promise** to allow myself to be who I want to be.
I **promise** to welcome the joy that life has to offer.
I **promise** to take care of my own needs by loving myself.
I **promise** to be gentle and nurturing to myself.
I **promise** to never again judge myself in hurtful ways.
I **promise** to do the things I like to do, without judgment.
I **promise** to find love in the world, starting with myself.
I **promise** to do whatever I can to stop the cycle of abuse.
I **promise** to love myself every minute of the day.
I **promise** to live in the here and now, not the past or future.
I **promise** to accept myself for who I am.
I **promise** to take good care of myself and to be loving always.
I **promise** to share my knowledge with others, to share my love.
I **promise** to be an ally for all other survivors who may have no voice.
I **promise** to hold my head up high and be proud of who I am.
I **promise** to make a difference so that abuse can be stopped.
I **promise** to live for today, while planning for tomorrow.
I **promise** to let the past go and to live my life with hope.
I **promise** to love, respect, nurture, and cherish myself always.

$\mathcal{M}$y Bill Of Rights

I believe that we should all have our own "Bill of Rights" to live by. These are mine:

Bill Of Rights For Survivors

1. **I have** a right to tell about the abuse—Breaking the Silence.
2. **I have** the right to cherish and love my own body.
3. **I have** a right to state when, how and with whom I want to have sex with, if at all.
4. **I have** a right to say *"NO"*.
5. **I have** a right to make my own decisions and choices.
6. **I have** a right to seek assistance and support if I want to.
7. **I have** a right to seek knowledge about abuse and learn how I can help stop it.
8. **I have** a right to feel safe, always.
9. **I have** a right to heal in my own unique way.
10. **I have** a right to be heard and understood.
11. **I have** a right to be treated with respect, honesty, and love from those around me.
12. **I have** a right to be loved for who I am.
13. **I have** a right to be happy and to make my life happier.
14. **I have** a right to decide how I want my life to be.
15. **I have** a right to control and change my own life.
16. **I have** a right not to feel guilty for the abuse. I am not to blame for someone else's actions, only my own.
17. **I have** a right to feel important, cherished, loved and most of all I have a right to be treated with dignity.

*M*y Wish For You

This book has taken you on an expedition that you will never travel again. There were many times I am sure that you wondered whether you could finish this journey. In my process, I too, worried at times about the same thing. The path I took which led me to write this book was intense and scary, but in the end, was exceedingly rewarding just as yours will be. I have discovered so many wonderful new friends, new ways to interact with others and a new me. I know I am not alone and that there are others who think, feel and believe as I do. My biggest joy was learning that I could speak out about the abuse and still be able to hold my head up high. I can look at myself in the mirror and say, "I truly love who I am and I know that I will never allow anyone to hurt me as I was hurt when I was abused". I have learned to stand up for myself, my family and most of all, my children.

My wish for you is that you too will find a new and loving person inside yourself. I believe we all have so much to offer others and ourselves. I also know that the world will not change unless we help to make it change. I hope that you will be able to speak out about abuse and help make a difference, not only in your own life, but possibly in the life of someone else who may not have a voice.

My wish for you is that you will create a world that is safe, loving and nurturing for yourself and those around you.

My wish for you is that you will be able to love those around you, especially the men in your life. I wish you peace, harmony, love and most of all friendship.

My wish for you is that you will remember that you are not alone. There are others who will want to help you, care for you and love you for who you are…even after learning you were abused.

Remember: With the help of this book, we survivors have completed a journey that has allowed us to explore new possibilities. We have given ourselves dignity by using journal exercises, affirmations, and the willingness to look inside and trust ourselves for answers. Many doors have now been opened to ourselves, family, friends and even the world. We have given ourselves the precious gift of knowing our TRUE SELVES. We have learned to love, forgive, nurture and accept who we are today. I believe you will continue to care for yourself each and every day of your life as you embrace new patterns of behaviour and continue to cherish the world around you. This is your life and you deserve to be happy. I end this book with sincere empathy, love and devotion to you and wish you peace and tranquility. Always be kind to yourself and remember you are not alone.

My Journey

At first, I couldn't see the road that I traveled,
It was too dark and scary.
At first, I stumbled and lost my way,
I had no real direction to follow.
At first, I cried and said "what's the use?"
I felt so alone and scared.
At first, I kept taking one step forward and three backwards,
I didn't know how to believe in myself.

At some point, I began to notice the road in front of me,
It wasn't quite as dark and scary as before.
At some point, I became better on my feet and kept walking,
I knew the road was bumpy and rough and that it would lead
me to places, I had never seen before.
At some point, I stopped crying long enough to hear other
peoples' voices, I began to notice I wasn't alone after all.
At some point, I took more steps forward than I did
backwards, I started to believe and to have faith in my abilities.
Now, I see the road ahead of me and I can look back to see
where I've come from without guilt or shame.
Now, I don't stumble very often, and when I do, I keep going.
I have a clear picture and understanding of the direction I want
to take with my life.
Now, I don't give up and say "what's the use?"
Instead, I look forward to the challenges that life has to offer
and I try to learn from my new experiences.
Now, I keep walking forward, only seldom do I look back to
reflect on the memories I left behind.

—Heather Mesaric

$\mathcal{R}$eferences

Page 3 – Government of Canada Statistics taken from the official website at: http://canada.justice.gc.ca/en/ps/fm/childafs.html

Page 4 – Health Canada quote taken from the official website at: http://www.hc-sc.gc.ca/hppb/familyviolence/html/nfntsnegl_e.html

Page 14 – Websters New Collegiate Dictionary, A Merrian-Webster 1980

Page 20 – Parker Palmer quote taken from the official website at: http://www.spiritedwoman.com/quotes.htm

Page 35 – Encarta World Dictionary

Page 221 – David Schwarts quote taken from the official website at: http://www.brainquote.com/quotes/quotes/d/davidjoseph165752.html

Page 225 – Nathaniel Branden quote taken from the official website at: http://www.brainquote.com/quotes/authors/n/nathaniel_branden.html

*S*uggested Reading

"The Spider Jones Story: Out Of The Darkness" by Spider Jones and Michael Hughes

I highly recommend this book. Spider Jones is a man who is determined to conquer his past. His story is about hardships, death, low self-esteem, bravery, determination, and personal growth on so many levels. It has an ending that will make you say...good for you, you deserve all the happiness in the world. Most all, his story provides the proof that personal dreams, do in fact, happen to those who go after them. I was at one of his speaking engagements and discovered he truly is a motivational speaker with a purpose to inspire others to believe in their dreams. He constantly states: "You Have to Believe to Achieve."

"The Little Engine That Could" by Watty Piper

I recommend this book because it helps the reader to believe that anything is possible, if you only believe that you can do it.

"The Big O" by Lou Page

This book helps you to explore your beliefs about your own sexuality. It helps to destroy the barriers which hinder you from having a positive understanding and acceptance of your own sexual needs.

"Creative Visualization" by Shakti Gawain

I first read this book so many years ago and yet I continue to re-read it often, especially when I need to be reminded that what we believe and think about, will manifest in our lives.

"The Power of Intention" by Dr. Wayne Dyer

Dr. Wayne Dyer has quite a few books in publication and this is one of my favourites. It deals with helping you to take the needed steps to change your life.

"Getting in the Gap" by Wayne Dyer

This book helps you to explore and answer questions in relationship to meditating in order to find inner peace with God. It has a CD disk which takes you through the process of meditating to music.

Contacting Author

If you or your organization would like to contact the Author for bookings, or to share your story of healing with her please email: icanheal@rogers.com

Please note: if you are emailing the Author you must put in the subject area of the text: It's Time To Heal and state subject matter examples: It's Time To Heal – booking, or It's Time To Heal – question, or It's Time To Heal – comment on book, or It's Time To Heal – sharing my story. The Author <u>will not open any correspondence that does not have - It's Time To Heal – and the subject matter</u>, in the subject area.

Or write to her at: Time To Heal Enterprises
                        61 Twenty-Sixth Street
                        Etobicoke, Ontario
                        M8V 3R8

Or visit her website: www.time-to-heal.com

Phone Numbers To Assist Those In Need:

The following are phone numbers which are toll free and most of them have 24 hours a day availability. If you need to find someone to talk to, you might be able to find the help you are looking for, by calling or looking up one of the following numbers or sites:

Kids Helpline Phone (Canada) – 1 800 668 6868
available in English or French

Child Help USA – 1 800 4 – A-Child (22 4453)

Rape Abuse & Incest National Hotline 1 800 656 HOPE (4673)

Child Abuse Hotline 1 800 252 2873

National Youth Crisis Hotline 1 800 442 HOPE (4673)

Youth Crisis Hotline (reporting child abuse and help for runaways
1 800 HIT HOME (448 4663)

National Domestic Abuse Hotline 1 800 799 SAFE (7233)

Websites To Look Up For Resources...

Search The Web – Child Abuse Hotline Canada or USA

You can look at the following links from this page in order to access information that might be helpful...

Kids in Trouble Help Page Hotline Numbers – Provides listing for several countries with phone numbers to call.
www.geocities.com/EnchantedForest/2910/hotlines.html
Stop It Now – Resources Guide – Victims and Survivors of Child Sexual Abuse – Provides numbers and connects you to your local service for help.
www.stopitnow.org/resourceguide/rg03_vicsurv.html

Childhelp Abuse Hotline – Childhelp USA
www.childhelpusa.org/programs_hotline.htm

Child Abuse – www.mcc.org/abuse/child_abuse/index.html

ISBN 1412062470-0